AF444937

How to be a Worship Songwriter

Declare Your Purpose
Discover Your Manifesto

STEPHEN ROBERT CASS

An imprint of Solid Walnut Music
15620S. 14th Place
Phoenix, AZ 85048
https://songs4god.net

Send feedback to feedback@songs4god.net

Copyright© 2023 by Stephen Robert Cass
All rights reserved by Solid Walnut Music,
who believes in the sanctity of copyright. It fuels
creativity and diversity, promotes free speech,
and helps our culture flourish.

Thank you for buying an authorized version of this book, and for not distributing, copying,
or reproducing it in any manner without written permission (except for brief quotes). You
are supporting Solid Walnut Music to continue to publish books the reader wants.

Printed in the United States of America

10 9 8 7 6 5 4 3 2 1

Library of Congress Cataloging-in-Publication Data
Cass, Stephen Robert
how to be a worship songwriter:
declaring your purpose and
discovering your manifesto
by Stephen Robert Cass.
1. Cass, Stephen Robert—Songwriting 2. Music publishing

ISBN 979-8-9855371-8-5 (pbk)
ISBN 979-8-9882198-1-1 (audio)
ISBN 979-8-9855371-9-2 (epub, ASIN)
ISBN 979-8-9882198-0-4 (pdf)

Scriptures taken from the
HOLY BIBLE, NEW INTERNATIONAL VERSION,
Copyright © 1973,1978, 1984
by International Bible Society.
Used by permission of Zondervan Publishing House.

All graphics in this book are the sole property of Solid Walnut Music, who reserves all rights.
Reproductions for commentary uses are permitted with acknowledgement to Song4God.net Media and
Stephen Robert Cass. Any reproduction for the purpose of commerce must have written permission.

Cover design: Songs4God.net Media
Interior layout: Formatted books.com
Content Editing: Jerry Bradley
Line and Copy Editing: Fresheyesproofreaders.com
Printing in the Unites States: IngramSpark and Amazon KDP

The names of individual products in this book are the sole property of their respective owners.

Significant discounts for bulk print and e-book sales are available
by emailing steve@songs4god.net or call (480) 773-3484

Contents

Titles by Stephen Robert Cass

The 5 Steps to Get Your Songs Heard
A Congregational Songwriting Plan

The Proverbs 27.17 Song Critique Method
The Power of Group Learning to Deliver Songs

Fishing in Church: How to Be a
Congregational Songwriter
*A blueprint for learning the craft of
congregational songwriting
and getting your songs heard*

The 5 Keys to a Clear Mix: Create YOUR Mix Philosophy
for Christian Artists, Songwriters, and Church Song Mixers

Establishing a Culture of Lead Worshipers:
How to Build a Worship Team
Everyone on the platform is a lead worshiper

The Harmony for Worship Project
Training Voices to Praise the Living God

Worship Songs and the Law
*How Churches Stay Legal
How Songwriters Get Paid*

For Dr. Chuck Fromm, who encouraged me
and many worship leaders to build songwriting
communities based on local song theology.

Introduction

THIS BOOK IS FOR ANYONE, young or old, who has heard the call from God to write songs. I will help you discover and declare your purpose in songwriting and show you a path forward. This manifesto shows an outline for a blueprint for writing songs for church. You will use specific and custom song craft education tools to get your songs heard in local churches and churches around the world by learning the ways of *congregational* songwriting.

You will no longer suffer with thoughts such as *"I'm not good enough,"* or *"The only way I can get my songs heard is to be a worship leader,"* or *"Nobody is going to listen to my songs,"* or *"There are no schools or teachers showing how to write songs for God."*

I am a worship leader and published songwriter. I will answer each one of these internal struggles. I will show you exactly how to get your songs heard by implementing an exciting new strategy based on *local song theology.* Are you interested? Then, give this short book a read.

There are other methods to serve God with your songwriting—as a solo artist, in a group ministry, or writing specific songs that God gave you—but, read on to discover how your service to God and people will be enhanced even more by learning the ways of congregational songwriting.

This book is the overview of how you and I will take this blueprint into the future of songwriting in church, into an era I call the *small-church congregational songwriting revolution*. Picture the preparation I am proposing:

- dedicated, purposeful spiritual and personal development;
- song craft education including custom tools especially prepared for congregational songwriting (which also includes time-honored songwriting construction techniques);
- next-level song crafting techniques;
  - *The Proverbs 27.17 Song Critique Method*;
  - rewriting;
  - co-writing;
- the formation of a faith-based songwriting community, *and;*
- the construction of a faith-based music publishing company (which is *firmly* symbiotic with the songwriting community).

… and see yourself answering God's call to write songs for him by using this new method.

You and I can take this system and tools of songwriting and experience a fulfilling and meaningful future in the *small-church congregational songwriting revolution*. I believe this era began with the explosion in the numbers of independent Christian songwriters and church songwriting communities over the last 40 years. And now, technology, this blueprint, and Christian Copyright Licensing International (CCLI) administration will continue to pave the way for *local song theology* for the next 40 years for our churches. And beyond.

All of this—the nuts-and-bolts of this songwriting construction method and how we ride together into this new songwriting era—is (or will be!) written in many books, videos, blogs, manuscripts, conversations, and curriculum culminating in the Songs4God.net Worship Songwriting Academy.

Take a look at the Table of Contents and flip through to the final chapter to see the curriculum for the academy to get an idea of the individual components of the songwriting system I fittingly call "The Proverbs 27.17 Small-Church Congregational Songwriting Revolution."

I have at least four books planned to flesh out this songwriting approach: the one you are reading (the first in the series) and *The 5 Steps to Get Your Songs Heard,* (the second in the series) are already available. The third and fourth in the series, *The Proverbs 27.17 Song Critique Method* and *Fishing in Church,* are well underway. All books are or will be available anywhere you like to purchase books. See https://books2read.com/stephenrobertcass or https://getyoursongsheard.com.

In case you didn't get this book for free from my website, go to https://getyoursongsheard.com and download it again (give it to a friend) so you can take advantage of a *deep* loyalty discount, not available anywhere else, good on any of my books or the courses at the academy.

To present this songwriting creation and distribution formula to the world, this book, *How to Be a Worship Songwriter,* gives an overview of the philosophy and the essential nuts and bolts.

The 5 Steps to Get Your Songs Heard makes this philosophy and method of congregational songwriting walk and ties the songwriting tools to it, while *The Proverbs 27.17 Song Critique Method* shows how song critique is a proactive exercise in this style of songwriting construction and song distribution system. *Fishing in Church* will be an all-encompassing library of the philosophy and tools, a true reference of the songwriting strategy, and will house the basic description of the curriculum of the Songs4God.net Worship Songwriting Academy.

This online academy will present detailed information and certify songwriters and administrators for this congregational songwriting revolution.

If you are interested, please sign up to get more information at https://worshipsongwritingacademy.com.

This book reveals the individual components of the songwriting formula and how they work to serve the whole. Each chapter will be a brief description of the primary tools—custom and common—and the passion needed to bring this philosophy and the songwriting academy to life.

The major thrust of *this* book is to show you, the songwriter, the formula of writing congregational worship songs, and how you can harness this for your ministry and share the glory of God in your community.

But first, I need to tell you what drove me to create such a system—my revelations, dreams, and hopes—so I can answer those questions that are in the front of your mind, like *"I'm not good enough."* I will show how you can eliminate the negative thoughts and myths associated with songwriting, plus how you fit into this body of like-minded songwriters.

How to be a **Worship** Songwriter

1

The Angst that Fueled a Ministry

"Your eyes saw my unformed body; all the days ordained for me were written in your book."

—Psalm 139:16

I TAUGHT MYSELF TO PLAY GUITAR when I was 12 years old. I had played and sung at church for more than 25 years when I had the most remarkable moment during my prayer time. I knew I had talent from God to sing and play music, but I felt truly lost when trying to *write* songs. Real songs, songs that last and that make a difference. Creating original guitar work was not a problem but my lyric writing read and sounded like *whining from some hurt creature*. I longed to be a skilled writer. I had tried a few times, but nothing seemed to stick. Or the result was … blah. So sappy and passionless.

One day in April of 1995, I cried out to God in prayer: *"Why, God, did you give me this wonderful ability to play and sing but not the ability to produce anything original?"* My mind seemed adrift and directionless because I knew in my core that God built me to serve him in song. I felt like a ship navigator without course direction and exhausted of the waves pushing me around.

Not long before that I had rededicated my life and music to the work of God, but depression and restlessness festered in me. Just a musician going through the motions of playing at church. I knew that I was missing the mark on who he wanted me to be. Desperate to understand more of my reason for being and not just continue to hide behind the six strings, I needed *any* direction that made sense.

I had been avoiding God, running away from him, and not actively seeking guidance. To be just a musician in the crowd at church was okay, but I wanted to contribute more. *What did God have in store for the rest of my musical life?* During this prayer time, God gave me a new direction—one which sort of shocked me. He told me the reason I had trouble writing songs. "You're not writing about me!"

Well, that doesn't make any sense, I thought. *"You know, Lord, that I am not any good at writing lyrics."* "You just stick to the music." And as my eyes darted toward the Bible, he said, "I've already taken care of the lyrics."

Wow. That message just hit me like a ton of bricks. Of course. Here it was, right in front of me. I had all the tools. I had the drive and passion for Jesus and longed to learn more about him and his plan for my life. Like someone who just received their dream job, I could sense the super-charge of potential energy inside like a compressed spring. I tingled from head to toe. This day was the beginning of a season that I am still in today.

I started writing songs like I had been creating them for years. And I wrote better lyrics than I thought I could. Not great, but the word of God is a lyric writer's delight! After that revealing day of prayer, I wrote or co-wrote enough good songs for two albums. I became the producer and publisher for four other songwriters and artists, created the Solid Walnut Music label, and went into the studio to record. We produced five albums and physically distributed our music to fifteen countries by 2004.

This was at the turn of the century, a time when my website returned the #1 result for the search term "Christian music publisher." Demo tapes and letters jammed my mailbox. Most of them said how desperate they were for someone to listen to their songs, and that I was their last hope.

I received similar questions in my travels at churches around the country. Is there no outlet for songwriters who have heard the call from God to write? They are left with the question: *What's next? What do I do with my songs?*

Or, most often I heard, *God gave me a song, now what?*

That was becoming a familiar theme for me, songwriters without direction. And you may be thinking, *well, that's between them and God to figure out.* Fair enough.

For songwriters called by God to write, there is the direction to learn more about your artistry and to become a solo or band performer. There is the direction to become a worship leader and to try out your songs on your congregation or find worship leader friends to share the songs. Or maybe you could take the plunge and move to Nashville to slave away in the music trenches to figure it out, whether your effort leads you to become an artist or a staff songwriter. Maybe enrolling in a songwriting school will help, you think. Some who are called are not musicians but just looking for an outlet for their lyrics.

In the middle of all this angst, and seeking my own direction, I wrestled with a similar but more personal question: *Am I doing what I have been called to do with my songwriting?* Or, *what would God have me do with this songwriting gift?*

Even in my chosen direction, solo performer and worship leader, there remained a nagging thought that I wasn't fulfilling my call. I realized over time what my actual call was—writing *congregational* worship songs.

So, you might be asking what brought me to that conclusion. Let me tell you this story through a combination of experience, myth busting, and ingenuity. Then I want to invite you to ask yourself *"Why wouldn't that conclusion suit me, too?"*

2

Five Solutions that Slay the Negatives

"You never change things by fighting the existing reality. To change something, build a new model that makes the existing model obsolete."

—Buckminster Fuller

IN MY CASE, I STARTED NOTICING the structure of songs sung at church in comparison to popular secular songs. There are repetitive songs at church, sometimes the same in popular music, but that's not it. What I mean is the comparison of how songs work regarding communication with people. What makes people like songs?

For example, I have since learned more about song viability and what that means to major music publishers when they talk about songs on the radio. They might promote a few songs that don't belong there, but by and large, they will only promote the most popular songs from their artists. Most of these songs become popular because they communicate well and stick in the mind of the listener.

Some points of radio viability include:

- Song length: 3-4 minutes. Don't overstay your welcome.
- Short intro: 8-12 seconds. Get to the song.
- Reach the first chorus in less than a minute. This chorus is what you want them to remember.
- Positive songs that aren't preachy or condescending.
- Emotional songs that tug at your heart and really connect with listeners.
- Hooky songs that get stuck in your head are songs with longevity.
- You don't want them to tune out before getting to the chorus.
- Get it professionally produced, mixed, and mastered (to present to a gatekeeper).
- Stay with the popular song format (Verse, Chorus, Verse, Chorus, Bridge, Chorus).

Now, the good points about radio viability that I believe apply to congregational songwriting:

- Song length: 3-4 minutes. Don't overstay your welcome.
- Short intro: 8-12 seconds. Get to the song.
- Reach the first chorus in less than a minute. This chorus is what you want them to remember.
- Positive songs that aren't preachy or condescending.
- Emotional songs that tug at your heart and really connect with listeners.

- Hooky songs that get stuck in your head are songs with longevity.

The other criteria, such as staying with the popular song format, don't necessarily apply. This is only the beginning of that conversation, which I will address in the book *Fishing in Church.* My point for bringing it up now is in regard to my calling, that is to write congregational worship songs. One thing common in well-written commercial songs and songs that prosper in churches are lyrics that *invite the listener in and tell a story.*

> *One thing that is common in well-written commercial songs and songs that prosper in churches are songs with lyrics that invite the listener and tell a story.*

Congregational songwriting takes this commercial viability a few steps deeper, and in a different direction, so we can determine *congregational* viability. In song critique sessions, we also ask questions like:

- Can the chorus stand alone?
- Is the lyric conversational?
- Is the song easy to sing by the untrained masses?
- Would you characterize the song as congregational? Why or why not?

This brings up an important point. Some reading this are going to think that I am leaning towards legalism for songs used in church. There are those who believe that God gives them a song or lyrics and that they are sacred and only meaningful when kept in their original form. I understand the sentiment, but those types of songs are not destined to be sung by the masses.

"The Holy Spirit is the ultimate songwriter, but he chooses to flow through us to express himself. The more adept we are at crafting His messages, the clearer they become."

John Chisum, songwriter, former publishing executive for Integrity Music and VP of Publishing for Star Song Media

Imagine if I were to stand up and sing, "Holy, holy, holy are you Lord God Almighty. You reach into my heart and my life and teach me your ways of love and life. Spirit, be with me and cleanse me. Cleanse me. You're so sweet to me, and I love you forever, forever, forever. Hallelujah, hallelujah. Spirit, stay with me now and always, amen, amen, amen," as a reflection of an extraordinarily personal and powerful time of prayer and devotion. Then imagine that afterward I were to mine some nuggets from that prayer of praise to create a song singable by a large group:

> Holy God Almighty
> Fill my heart and life with your ways
> Spirit, cleanse and be with me
> Stay with me all of my days
> Hallelujah, Hallelujah!
> Holy God Almighty
> **© 2020 Stephen Robert Cass**

... now I would be sharing my inspiration in a way that others could join in and sing. I would never tell you that the crafted version of my prayer was better than when I got up to sing that original free-form prayer. But like the above quote from John Chisum, enjoy becoming adept at crafting a clear message for others to hear so they can join in and sing if they are so moved. And it *will* move them as you distill and amplify this powerful inspiration.

Maybe your song is a personal reflection, and you don't intend to share it. That's ok. Many songs start that way. You can decide the direction of your song. There may be times we want to use that sort of free-form, in-the-moment spiritual connection time in a church service, or to only sing the song in your personal prayer time.

But there are times for people to sing in one loud voice to their King. We sing together with our hearts in unison to praise our God and to build our faith. This book is about crafting worship songs to be sung by the masses.

♫ ♫ ♫

So, this first portion of the chapter told you a bit about my experience in learning about the nature of songs and the research into how songs are effective. Next, I'm going to show you how critical myth busting was in the development of my songwriting ministry and how essential it will be for your ministry. But I am not going to only bust each myth. I am going to show you the solutions to them, and how the solutions begin by aligning with Jesus' mission to the church.

I want to show you the mind shift that took place for me and convinced me to dedicate my life to congregational songwriting. My dedication to it has fostered a passion beyond my own songwriting. This fresh insight has ignited my heart to show you how to write consequential and meaningful songs for your local church. Read how each of the following negatives are transformed into a solution, beginning with how Jesus calls each of us. I encourage you to take the actions you read in the solutions today to begin or to continue your songwriting ministry.

NEGATIVE #1: I'M NOT GOOD ENOUGH

You know, I never dreamed I would become a successful songwriter. But now I have 70+ songs published in my CCLI catalog, with some of them being sung all over the planet. However, there are times when I still feel like I am not good enough, and I go through "imposter syndrome," that feeling that I will be exposed as a fraud.

Let me stop another thought that may be going through your head. No, I am not getting rich with these songs, but I do make pretty good coffee money! I got my songs "out there" and I feel good about that.

I still feel God calling me to dig deeper to use my talent. And not just my songs, but to show you how I have gotten them placed. God has been working in me through the years and is showing me an advanced way for us to get our songs used in our local churches and beyond to the wider world.

> *If God has called you to write songs, I have a message for you. Whether you are young or old, an experienced writer or not.*

And the local church and community are the priority.

So, I *am* good enough. So are you. Whether you are young or old, an experienced writer or not. If God has called you to write songs, I have a message for you. The quest God has me on uses my experiences in songwriting, studying song construction and placement, and leading worship to create a path going forward for you to write songs that connect people with Jesus. Songs that will make a difference in their lives.

> *But this is not about me or my fabulous theory on how to write songs. It is about empowering you and re-igniting local song theology.*

The songs will come from the grassroots and the experiences of the people in our congregations.

But this is not about me or my fabulous theory on how to write songs. It is about empowering you and re-igniting *local song theology.* I want to amplify your songwriting skill set and align your ministry with the power of the Holy Spirit so you can write songs that tell the story of how God is moving in the people of your community. Celebrate the victories, experiences, struggles, and tragedies and sing psalms, songs of lament, songs of praise, and inspired songs to God with your local church family.

> *"Let the message of Christ dwell among you richly as you teach and admonish one another with all wisdom through psalms, hymns, and songs from the Spirit, singing to God with gratitude in your hearts."*
>
> **Colossians 3:16**

I am not inventing good songwriting, I am inventing the *connection* between great songwriting technique and great worship, using both expected and custom tools.

> *I have discovered the connections between good song craft and theology and worship and music. I will highlight them and the tools specifically created for them in this book.*

I have discovered the connections between good song craft and theology and worship and music. Songwriting education today does not address the unique setting where people come to praise God. No songwriting education you could find pays attention to the need of songwriters that are distinctly called to communicate the Gospel of Peace. I will highlight these critical connections and the tools specifically created for them in this book.

And so, *you* are good enough. No experience? Start reading my material and getting together with like-minded songwriters. This pathway has never been available and can change your songwriting future. Do you have some experience or success writing songs? Bring your insights and skills and discover the unique pathway for the congregational songwriter.

At times, we may wonder what it is all about. And being called by God to write songs for him can be a lonely existence where negative thoughts that *I'm not good enough* can easily creep in, stifling creativity. I just read a post from a friend of mine telling of his journey to make it big. He said, "The best thing to do is enjoy the journey. Give it your best. Don't think you have failed if you don't reach the stars. Just write your best and leave the rest to God."

I want to expose why we often have misconceptions regarding the road to "making it big" when writing songs for God. All of us, every one of us, who strive to "be somebody" in songwriting, end up somewhat disappointed because our measuring stick is human effort to achieve spiritual goals. We have our shortcomings as humans and can't design pure spiritual goals, I get that. But combining our shortcomings with what we think is some sort of song ministry can often take us on a fantasy tour. If we don't reach a certain level of success, we think that we have somehow failed. We think that "success" is getting a record deal or being out on stage in front of thousands or getting a hit song recorded. There are two levels of justification going on between our ears:

1. We think we will reach some sort of nirvana when these things happen, and
2. Somehow, we believe that we can work hard at something for six months or a year, and this is enough for us to make our "break".

The people at the top of the songwriting and music game (according to the measurement of men and women) put in massive, massive effort to get to these positions. Your year-long, full-time investment is wonderful, but it doesn't come close to the efforts expended by the professionals who make a living at it, and sometimes slog in the unseen trenches for years before they get any sort of break.

To measure spiritual achievement by human standards and metrics is a recipe for disappointment, and Negative #1 *I'm not good enough* is one of the results from indigestion. It is almost impossible to forget about human metrics, though, and that is understandable.

But what if you aligned your purpose in songwriting with God's purpose of telling the story of the Gospel of Peace to the world? Let me share with you a concept that changed my way of thinking about songwriting. All the previous angst of human measurement is up against the *real* reason I believe God wants to use your writing gift. I believe it aligns with God's will for all of us who have been called to write songs.

It is a concept I call *Fishing in Church.*

But what if you aligned your purpose in songwriting with God's purpose of telling the story of the Gospel of Peace to the world?

SOLUTION#1: FISHING IN CHURCH

There's a reason Jesus chose the people who followed him. Some of them were deeply lost in life and needed his lifeboat. But most were just regular people trying to make their way in life. One of the things the core group of disciples had in common, though, was their focus on a particular task: that of catching fish for a living. For those of you who like to fish, what is the first picture that comes to your mind? Actually catching a fish, right? If you have caught a fish, you know what I mean.

Jesus knew what drove that core group. He knew that there was a forever-picture in their minds: A thrill of the chase, an obsession with it, and that this vision was the quarry that sustained their lives. After filling their nets to the brim and proving to them that he was the Master Provider, he told them they were just getting started. *"Don't be afraid; from now on you will fish for people."* (Please read this story now in Luke 5:1–11)

Jesus fills their nets

Even if you don't like to fish, I think you can visualize it. There are those who are so focused on a task that they will do whatever it takes to get the outcome they are working to achieve. The Father uses this drive within us to draw us close and align us with the Son to complete our mission on Earth. This same yearning keeps you, the songwriter—or you who are called to mix live sound at church or make demos and support Christian music—working for people and for God.

Jesus is calling you and me to fish for people. He recognizes the drive we have because he put it there! So, rather than wallow in the conversation going around in our brains that our songwriting is without guidance and direction, let me offer up this statement: We have a calling. Those of us called by God to write are indeed called by Jesus to use our talent to fish for people. Just as if Jesus began talking of food and you realized that you were hungry. Hungry for the Bread of Life.

And where do people gather who seek to know him? They come to homes and multi-purpose school rooms and church buildings and sing together about the God they love. *This* is our mission field. We are called to fish in church.

It is not about "singing to the choir," it is about bringing heartfelt theology in song to people yearning to learn more about *God's* mission to us: To give us his everlasting comfort, his love, and salvation for our lives. He made that promise clear by giving us his one and only Son, that anyone who might believe in him should have everlasting life. Everlasting life, the fullness of life, the abundant life that begins here and now according to Jesus in John 10:10, "*... I have come that they may have life and have it to the full.*"

The desire of God the Father and Jesus the Son is for us all to find *shalom* (completeness, wholeness, health, peace, welfare, tranquility, prosperity, perfectness, fullness, rest, harmony, and the absence of agitation or discord) according to John 14:27.

> *"Peace I leave with you; my peace I give you. I do not give to you as the world gives. Do not let your hearts be troubled and do not be afraid."*
> **John 14:27**

That is *God's* story. That is *our* story to tell in song.

Jesus revealed a new model for thinking about life which made the old way obsolete.

♬ ♬ ♬

Join me in discovering your songwriting future. Get rid of all thoughts that you are not worthy or good enough. Listen to the call God has placed on your heart and declare your new purpose is song ministry for the people of God. Decide your new mission is to learn the unique pathway of *congregational* songwriting and to fish in church.

None of us are good enough. That is why we have a Savior. We are all saved for eternity by the grace of God but saved so we can do good works that feed, clothe, and uplift the church body. You will find songwriters of every level in the *small-church congregational songwriting revolution*, ready to do great works through their songwriting gift.

NEGATIVE #2: THE ONLY WAY I CAN GET MY SONGS HEARD IS TO BE A WORSHIP LEADER

Or, to get my songs to a worship leader. I am a worship leader, so I understand. Let me say that our first job as worship leaders, really our only job, is to lead the congregation to the foot of the cross. We amplify the message of the pastor or the church. Or, as one of the most revered worship leaders on the planet, Rick Muchow, planting worship leader of Rick Warren's Saddleback Church of Lakeside, CA, told us in a 2013 Worship Leader Magazine songwriting conference workshop:

> *"The job of a great pastor is to bring the fire of the Holy Spirit to the people. The job of a great worship leader is to **light** the fire."*

Worship leaders have that task and other relationship and music duties that keep us quite busy. We need to write songs in our down time. Sometimes we may have the opportunity to share our songs, but songwriting worship leaders are not in the majority.

One thing you might think is that your worship leader will take the time to listen and encourage you in your songwriting. Some may, but many will not have the time. Worship leaders often don't have the bandwidth or the expertise to help you with your songs.

Today, I want you to realize that your worship leader is *not* a gatekeeper for your songs. They have more important work to do. You need dedicated feedback from experienced songwriters.

SOLUTION #2: THE SMALL-CHURCH CONGREGATIONAL SONGWRITING REVOLUTION

But worship leaders and pastors *are* hungry for fresh, relevant songs. The Songs4God.net Worship Songwriting

Academy presents a new model for songwriting, the *small-church congregational songwriting revolution*, which addresses the relationships between the songwriter, the songwriting organization, and the worship leader. This new model is making the old one obsolete. Dedicated congregational songwriters will create quality songs, and faith-based songwriting organizations will deliver those songs to small and mid-sized churches.

I will describe the design of this process, the community of like-minded songwriters and the songwriting organizations, in Chapters 6 and 7. The leaders of the group can introduce your songs to local pastors and worship leaders.

NEGATIVE #3: NOBODY IS GOING TO LISTEN TO MY SONGS

This plaintive notion covers a multitude of false hope. It is also vague. But I get it, I really do. It is the thinking that since we are not good enough—we are not in the "in crowd"—that no one will think twice about listening to our songs or reading our lyrics, so why try?

Have you ever felt the sting of rejection? Ahhh! I have and it is no fun. Many of us songwriters have tried a very futile method in the past that only feeds this Negative #3 monster *nobody is going to listen to my songs*. Songwriters keep doing it today, only to set themselves up for rejection. We labor over our songs and then send them, unsolicited, to music publishers. And then we hear nothing back from them. Even follow-up phone calls don't bear much fruit.

Because creativity is so connected to our hearts, many of us then feel that sting of rejection. And this can lead to the attitudes of *"Why even try?"* or, *"What do they know about me?"* or, *"I'll just strike out somehow on my own."*

The reality is that music publishers need sure-thing songs. They make deals when there is money to be made, just like any other successful business.

Mike Harland, director of Lifeway Worship, seeks new Christian songs for a living. But he sees the great misconception, and how passionate and desperate songwriters want to get their songs out there at any cost, yet choose to not seek a higher level of song craft:

> *"Songwriters have this fantasy that if they can just get their songs in front of the right people, then they'll get a cut or get a contract, and it just doesn't work that way. Spend energy seeking attention for your songs by raising the level of your songwriting so that you write songs that are worthy of attention."*
>
> **Mike Harland, Director**
> **of Lifeway Worship**

How can we reasonably conclude that people will listen to our songs when we present songs that aren't worthy of attention?

When these feelings come along, I understand. But, what this can lead us to is either analysis paralysis or the idea that the music industry is full of bad people. Sure, there are bad people in the industry, but the vast majority are great people like you and me, just trying to get along in life.

Don't feel jaded. Understand that rejection is a part of the songwriting game. Grammy-nominated songwriter Jason Blume has written songs that have sold more than 50,000,000 copies. It took him 16 years as a professional songwriter before he started making any extra money. He has written over 1,000 songs and received over 10,000 rejections over those many years.

Jason Blume has written over 1000 songs and received over 10,000 rejections over 16 years. How does this translate to your chances as a part-time songwriter?

How does this translate to your chances as a part-time songwriter? Read about this and similar stories in the second book of this series, *The 5 Steps to Get Your Songs Heard.* Go to https://getyoursongsheard.com or https://books2read. com/stephenrobertcass.

SOLUTION #3: I KNOW SOMEONE WHO *WILL* LISTEN TO YOUR SONGS

I know someone who will listen to your songs. The Songs4God.net Worship Songwriting Academy presents a new model which, again, makes this old one obsolete. It is the outlet each one of us needs, just for the sake of being heard. It serves that purpose, but it is more than that. It is a way to grow as a songwriter because you will get *proper* feedback. The price you will pay for this type of service is to learn to grow "thick skin", but it will give you the tools you need to make your songs worthy of attention. Sound interesting? This is going to require you to learn the art of song critique.

Learning the art of song critique is just as important as learning how to present a lyric in a symmetrical song form. It is probably more important. The critique of a song is for two distinct purposes in our songwriting world:

- the betterment of the song and the songwriter, and
- the advancement of the songwriting community.

Nothing else. This is not a song contest. This is not a situation where a slate of judges gives the nod to more experienced songwriters so they win. Your song will have a full evaluation of its content against the strong criteria of a good congregational song. But most importantly, you will receive a beneficial feedback *report* designed to help you become an expert songwriter.

> *Learning the art of song critique is just as important as learning how to present a lyric in a symmetrical song form. It is probably more important.*

Song critique is an integral part of The Proverbs 27.17 Small-Church Congregational Songwriting Revolution process. We need it in order to provide the best songs possible, so we present our strongest songs to the world but also to accelerate the learning process. It is a valuable community exercise that will bear great fruit for the individual, the songwriting community, and your local church body.

So, there *is* someone who will listen to your songs. Learn to revel in the song critique process. This will change *everything.* It will change your songwriting future. Read more about this method later in this book under *The Songwriting Tools of the Proverbs 27.17 Congregational Small-Church Revolution.*

NEGATIVE #4: THERE ARE NO SCHOOLS OR TEACHERS SHOWING HOW TO WRITE SONGS FOR GOD

Meaning there is no one specifically educating Christians in the ways of writing Christian songs, or there are no songwriting schools acknowledging that a genre of Christian songwriting exists.

There are stellar songwriting teachers available who have won awards and have had success in the market. They are indispensable resources for our learning journey. We should embrace them.

But these teachers will not show you the specialized needs of writing songs of faith for faith communities. They may show you impressive structure, communication, and form; that will be very useful, but they cannot show the unique considerations of spiritual settings and the connection between great song craft and worship.

There are also some wonderful books written by famous worship leaders and songwriters. They tell of their unique experiences and good ideas for relationships in church and leadership dynamics on worship teams. But sharing the technical aspect of songwriting for church is something not written about. There are, however, a few outstanding examples. Look up Robert Sterling, Paul Baloche, and Krissy Nordhoff.

SOLUTION #4: PRESERVING LOCAL SONG THEOLOGY

But the Proverbs 27.17 Small-Church Congregational Songwriting Revolution is a new process. It is not a series of books about my experiences, although they are there to help show how this can work for you. This is a system for getting *congregational-style* songs published for local churches and the wider world.

It teaches spiritual development, discipleship, specific song craft education, as well as songwriting community and music publishing disciplines and is part of a BHAG—big, hairy, audacious goal. That goal is to preserve the practice of local song theology, which is *to allow the songs of your congregation to reflect how God is moving in your community,* and to become the champion for local worship songwriters to get their songs heard. This led to the establishment of the Songs4God.net Worship Songwriting Academy.

Why do I want to help spread local song theology? Because there are wonderful songs in our church communities today, songs that come from the music industry. But I believe many of our songs should come from the grassroots of the church—you.

Why is this "preserving" local song theology? Because this is how the modern era of songwriting in church began. There are many wonderful examples.

Calvary Chapel is a church that began in California in the late '60s, founded by Pastor Chuck Smith. You might have heard about the hippie church, and there's even a movie out about that experience right now in 2023—with Kelsey Grammer playing Pastor Chuck Smith and Jonathan Roumie playing hippie preacher Lonnie Frisbee—called *The Jesus Revolution.* The Jesus Movement of the 60's and '70s is credited as the beginning of the Christian rock music industry in the United States.

The musicians of Calvary Chapel wrote songs locally for their churches and the songs were organized as Maranatha! Music. After a while it had become quite large.

By 1975, Pastor Chuck Smith contacted his nephew, Chuck Fromm, to come and lead the music production and the musicians at Calvary Chapel. Dr. Fromm remained as the president of Maranatha! Music for the next 25 years and received the Lifetime Achievement Award from the Gospel Music Association in 1990. He founded Worship Leader Magazine in 1992.

(You will read more about Dr. Fromm, local song theology, and how he has influenced me and other worship leaders later in this book.)

Chuck Fromm, left, and his uncle Chuck Smith

The Maranatha! Music song catalog became one of the very first, and one of the most important Praise and Worship song catalogs ever built. It is one of the most active music catalogs on the CCLI charts.

Hillsong church began in Sydney, Australia in 1983. They didn't start their church thinking that they would plant churches worldwide and have their songs sung in churches across the world. No, they started as a small church who followed a call from God to record their songs and distribute them to their local community. *That's* where it starts. At the grass roots.

Hillsong Publishing had such enormous success that they created a music publishing method and distributed their songs around the world and became one of the most active catalogs on the CCLI charts in New Zealand and Australia, and ultimately, the United States.

Elevation Church released a song titled *Give Me Faith* in 2013. The songwriting team wrote it in alignment with a sermon series to help their people respond when they felt their lives were falling apart (listen to the story at https://www.youtube.com/watch?v=wW8-pzWOspE). It inspired them then, as it inspires us today, to allow God to work through them in spite of their weaknesses, to allow the Holy Spirit to reign in their lives (2 Corinthians 12:9). The song has grown from a local North Carolina church encouragement and grassroots faith story to one among many famous songs from them now sung in churches around the world.

Until the success of Calvary Chapel, Hillsong, Elevation Church and others—ministries like Spirit and Song from New Zealand, The Vineyard movement, Michael W. Smith, worship leaders Chris Tomlin, Matt Redman, David Crowder and Passion City Church, The Upper Room, Gateway Worship, and so many more—the record industry wouldn't touch Christian music. Now record companies have entire divisions dedicated to the genre. Mostly, because they are making money, not because they care about spreading the gospel.

But, I am not writing this to trash the music industry. We have some great worship songs for our churches now because of them. But this is my point: Great local song theology flourished in churches around the world *before* the record industry made these churches and artists household names. Also my point: Great local song theology will flourish *without* the record industry. Or, at the very least, our great local songs will live alongside it.

This rise of popular music industry songs in our churches has been wonderful. But think about the inspiration for each one of them. *God made himself known through these songs, based on the stories and experience of people, inspired by messages from local pastors. The local songwriter molded these stories and gave them back to their community to honor and praise God.*

It is through *local song theology* that we witness God moving in our communities. God speaks through the specific connections between the local songwriter, the people, and their pastor. We can sing wonderful and glorious songs to God that magnify our connections with him *even more so* because we are celebrating local victories and teachings.

It is important that the music in your church aligns with the message of your pastor and are not just some popular song selections. Popular worship songs are genuine and heartfelt. But most of the songs are about local victories and learnings, and we sing of another community's victory and experience when we sing a popular song. Nothing wrong with that, but how much more could a church community celebrate and grow spiritually if they were singing songs about their *own* victories and teachings?

I am not suggesting that we promote sub-par songs apart from the music industry. I *am* suggesting that we can write songs just as good and *better*. They will be *better* because of their heartfelt and homespun connections that will magnify the praise and worship of the people to their God.

They will be better because you will know, through this custom congregational songwriting blueprint, the deep connections found in remarkable song craft technique that are inspired by wisdom and discipline *especially aligned with the calling of the congregational songwriter.* Your songs will have depth because they will draw from your personal connection with God, and they join with the principles of the heart of worship as taught by Jesus.

This is great news for the church body and how you can use your songwriting gift. But it is also great news for you because this new method of learning to write congregational songs has a direct audience: your congregation, or local congregations. This songwriting approach is designed so peers *will* listen to your songs, give you feedback to make them better, and make sure the best of them are published.

So, there *is* a school out there dedicated to showing you the ways of congregational songwriting, the Songs4God. net Worship Songwriting Academy. It does not exist as a place to gather and share songs, although there will be a community associated with it. The academy is designed to educate songwriters on the disciplines needed to write and release worship songs *worthy of the attention of worship leaders and pastors.*

You can help preserve local song theology and be a songwriter in the small-church revolution.

WHY IS IT THE *SMALL-CHURCH REVOLUTION?*

Most of the popular songs used in worship today come from large churches, and while they are beautiful, powerful, and worshipful, there are many, many small- and mid-sized churches that need to benefit from their *own* local song theology. The message from the music industry is that *you must use our songs.*

Larger churches often dedicate significant time and resources to a songwriting community. Most pastors and worship leaders of small- and mid-sized churches don't have that luxury. As a worship leader myself, I can tell you how much time and effort the role takes. Most church ministry leaders must concentrate on establishing a culture of worship and maintaining relationships. They just don't have the bandwidth to handle yet another task.

When smaller churches do decide to start a songwriting ministry, they often fail to set achievable goals. This can cause them to fall short of meeting many expectations because of their need to concentrate on the fundamental ministries of the church.

Therefore, I propose we create songwriting communities *outside* of any church so that these associations can serve multiple local congregations with fresh songs. Songwriters of any size church can band together, creating the opportunity for songwriters from smaller churches that otherwise would never have the opportunity to be heard.

This can be done with leadership dedicated to becoming champions for the songwriters and for local song theology. It is a partnership between songwriters, pastors, and worship leaders. I will talk more about this blueprint in the chapters

The Faith-based Songwriting Community and *The Faith-based Music Publishing Company.*

NEGATIVE #5: BUSTING THE NASHVILLE MYTH

The next part of this feeling that no one is showing others how to write Christian songs stems from what I call the Nashville Myth. Ahem. Myths were made to be busted. So, here goes.

This myth is not some passive-aggressive swipe at the town or the music industry. No, I know wonderful people there who work hard to feed their families. The myth has to do with how you view songwriting success, and how too many of us believe that the gate for our songs is Nashville.

There is only one famous songwriter in Nashville I know of who is encouraging songwriters to write worship: Dove Award-nominated Krissy Nordhoff, who is a staff songwriter for Essential Music Publishing. God bless her efforts and please look her up. She is spending a lot of time helping Christian songwriters.

The record companies are not in business to help you become a better songwriter. Do you remember in the last chapter I told you my mailbox used to be flooded with unsolicited song demos and letters? Some letters were well-written and calmly asked me to listen to their music, but many of them were from *desperate* songwriters who begged me to listen to their stuff. They would write words like I was their only hope. Well, think about that load of demos and multiply by 10. Record companies get these unsolicited requests *every day.*

This is not the way to introduce yourself and your songs to the music industry, yet songwriters do it all the time. Why? Record companies are in business to make money with songs, not help you invest in a songwriting future. No one will listen to your songs in order to give you the feedback you need to become a sought-after writer.

> *Record companies are in business to make money with songs, not help you invest in a songwriting future.*

Besides, getting introductions to the music industry is all about personal contact. Do you remember earlier in this chapter my reference to Grammy-nominated songwriter Jason Blume? And do you remember how long it took him literally pounding the pavement before the music industry recognized his talent (16 years)? That is what it takes.

Songwriting artists may be able to make successful song pitches to the music industry if they already have a track record of song placements.

It is not the same for songwriters called by God—those not in Nashville and not previously successful. The music industry doesn't care that you want to write songs that tell of his glory.

THE SOLUTION #5: BLOOM WHERE YOU ARE PLANTED

Writing worship songs for church carries a different sort of importance than any other type of song. Consider blooming where Creator God planted you. There is a reason you are *who* you are and *where* you are. Psalm 139 tells us that *Abba Father* knew you before you were formed in your mother's womb. Woven throughout the Bible are examples of ordinary, imperfect people being used by God in extraordinary ways where they were. He's going to use you, too.

Some people travel to do the work of God. Do that if you're so called. But don't think you have to move to fulfill your calling as a worship songwriter. There are plenty of churches in your hometown. This is where you're needed. See, God has you where he needs you. Unless you hear the call to move distinctly or just decide to move because you want a change of scenery, consider the Apostle Paul's advice to the Corinthian believers:

> *"Nevertheless, each person should live as a believer in whatever situation the Lord has assigned to them, just as God has called them…in the situation they were in when God called them."*
>
> **1 Corinthians 7:17, 24**

Paul was telling them—as well as us today—that wisdom should rule. He recognized that seeking contentment and productivity in our current situation and allowing God to work through us is true wisdom, and how we will best prosper.

Throw away the obsolete thoughts that you need to be somewhere else. Rather than fussing elsewhere, look for understanding and insight where you are planted.

Paul was telling them—as well as us today—that wisdom should rule. He recognized that seeking contentment and productivity in our current situation and allowing God to work through us is true wisdom, and how we will best prosper.

Rather than thinking that someone in the music industry is going to "discover" you (the industry moved on from that decades ago), use your energy to define your local ministry. Replace this *Fear of Missing Out* with the transparency of how God views you and your ministry, and how he has created a different path for you than you may think.

Contrary to what they say, the grass is *not* always greener on the other side. Take direct aim to fulfill your call to write songs for God—wherever you are.

I am establishing a songwriting system to help you shape your ministry. Not to make money, but to do my part and spread the gospel of Jesus Christ. My BHAG is not to create a single songwriting organization for smaller churches, but to enable you to create your own songwriting organization in your community. For your sake and for the health of the church.

Are you with me?

3

Serve the Body of Christ with Your Gifts

"But in fact God has placed the parts in the body,
every one of them, just as he wanted them to be. If
they were all one part, where would the body be?
As it is, there are many parts, but one body."

— 1 Corinthians 12:18-20

FINDING OUT WHAT MAKES YOU TICK will help you identify not only your strengths and weaknesses, but also your passions. Understanding your passions and strengths and recognizing your gifts will produce the best results, not only for your benefit but for the benefit of those around you. You will be better prepared to serve our King and stay joyful in your tasks.

How would you rate your songwriting skills? What are your spiritual gifts that can help in the songwriting process? Can you lead other like-minded songwriters to accomplish mutually passionate tasks? Are you always ready to learn? Are you willing to help others learn and grow? How does your personality inform you about the way you interact with people best? What personal experiences have molded you into who you are? Can you take some cues from your life to help other songwriters succeed? What aspects of songwriting are you good at, and what aspects could use some input?

How would you rate your songwriting skills? What are your spiritual gifts that can help when writing songs?

Answering these questions about your love of writing words and making music will help set you on the right path in the creation process. A songwriter is often better at writing lyrics than melodies, or the opposite. It is good to identify which of these is more your strength so you can pay attention to improving the mechanical/academic and spiritual aspects of the other skill.

I found the perfect songwriting personality test online (the link is below). It confirmed some suspicions I had about my own strengths and weaknesses. I really appreciated the feedback that opened my eyes to the different facets of song construction (hearing/prophetic, concept, structure, melody, producer/track, chords/arranging). I hope you will take the personality test; I think you will like it as much as I did.

I dive more deeply into the songwriting personality test in Chapter 5 in the section on co-writing. The test will help you get to know yourself and your fundamental songwriting abilities; it will expose your true strengths so you know how to contribute when you co-write songs. You will realize that you can be proactive and offer what you do well to a songwriting team.

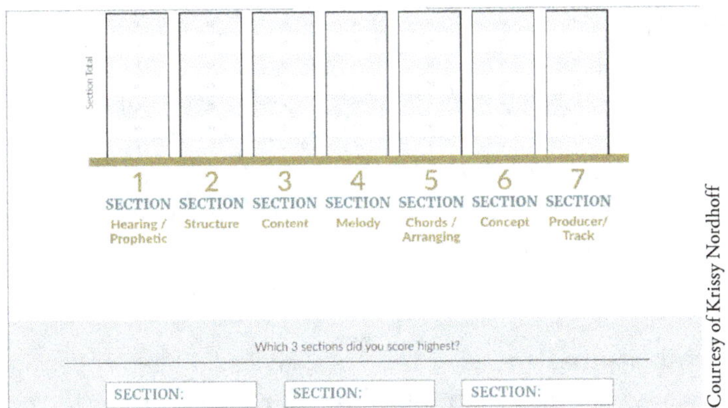

**Songwriting Personality Test
(Extended Version) from Krissy Nordhoff**

Spend time now to learn about yourself by taking the Songwriter Personality test at https://krissynordhoff.com/test. Be sure also to take the extended version. This is a steppingstone to help master your skills and become excited about sharing your songwriting proficiencies.

There are other exciting tests that can enlighten and help you understand who you are and how you react to people and the world around you.

WHAT IS YOUR S.H.A.P.E?

Rick Warren, pastor and author of *The Purpose Driven Life*, coined the acronym S.H.A.P.E. It stands for spiritual gifts, heart, abilities, personality, and experience. It is a great model that will help you to better understand yourself and to be in tune with how you can help yourself, your family, friends, and co-workers. It can help you to discover your part in the body of Christ and learn better how God has called you.

S

> *For just as each of us has one body with many
> members, and these members do not all have the
> same function, so we in Christ, though many
> form one body, and each member belongs to all
> the others.*
>
> **Romans 12:4, 5**

Spiritual gifts. If you are a leader, then lead diligently. If you teach, give it your utmost. Give your all according to the skills that God has given you.

> *So Christ himself gave the apostles, the prophets,
> the evangelists, the pastors and teachers, to equip
> his people for works of service, so that the body of
> Christ may be built up until we all reach unity
> in the faith and in the knowledge of the Son of
> God and become mature, attaining to the whole
> measure of the fullness of Christ.*
>
> **Ephesians 4:11-13**

Do you lead ministries? Are you a person who starts projects with others? It is important that you spend a moment and read Ephesians chapter 4 right now. The quoted verse cannot do justice to the context in which Paul writes. In this chapter, he tells his friends how crucial it is for all in Christ to mature so that we build each other up and are not swayed by those who preach another gospel.

(Today, we may not be tempted by another gospel, but rather by cleverness or deceit that leads us down a path of selfishness, so that we are serving self rather than the body).

The scripture quoted at the beginning of this chapter is 1 Corinthians 12:18-20. We know from these verses and the others in this section that God intends us to serve each other. We can't serve properly unless we understand our gifts.

H

Heart. What makes you passionate? Our greatest passion is often connected to our deepest pain. I encourage you to search your heart, as well as your history to see where God and the body of Christ may need you. A scripture quote that comes to mind is from Romans 8:28:

> *And we know that in all things God works for the good of those who love him, who have been called according to his purpose.*

In my opinion, this verse means very little without knowing the context around it. In the previous verse, Paul writes about how the Holy Spirit helps us in our weakness. The more we align ourselves with the Holy Spirit, the more we can understand that we have been called to serve God, and the more we recognize how our strengths and weaknesses can serve the body of Christ on earth. We can know beyond any doubt that we are indeed chosen to glorify God, and he is well pleased with us when we exercise our gifts for him.

We can know beyond any doubt that we are indeed chosen to glorify God, and he is well pleased with us when we exercise our gifts for him.

A

Your abilities. Take an inventory of how you are bent as a person and the skills you have or want to acquire. Your inventory should include things for which you have an affinity and your preferences. Make a plan to gain the skills you desire so you can fulfill your calling and serve. This can be anything from writing up your resume to signing up for online classes, or making plans to enroll for higher education.

P

Personality. There are many helpful personality tests available, and you should take advantage of multiple. One evaluation may emphasize an area that others do not. It is important to get a broad understanding of the different personality evaluation philosophies out there. Some personality tests might lean more toward leadership and team building, while others might be better suited toward finding happiness and fulfillment. Below is a short list of tests. If you are not interested in any of these, let Google be your friend. There are many out there.

- Spiritual Gifts- https://giftstest.com/test
- Myers-Briggs- https://www.16personalities.com/free-personality-test
- Enneagram- https://www.truity.com/test/enneagram-personality-test
  - https://www.thepersonalitylab.org/
- Sparktype- https://sparketype.com

Here is the url to an article that summarizes twenty-three personality tests: https://www.workstyle.io/best-personality-test

E

Experience. In line with your abilities, write down everything you have done in your life. Include things like work, volunteer events, mission trips, summer jobs, accomplishments, awards, etc. You have gained experience that *no one* has but you. Make this life experience work towards a better understanding of who you are and what you offer.

4

The Ways of the Holistic Songwriter

"A deep desire to communicate inspires songwriting."

—Bono

NOW THAT YOU KNOW more about yourself, your abilities and your skill set … now that you know what drives you and how to slay the negative self-messages about writing songs for God … now that you understand more about how you interact with others, your leadership qualities and collaboration skills … and now that you understand that the music industry doesn't exist to grant you favors, you can better prepare yourself to take your life forward in the best direction.

You can harness these revelations and your deep desire to learn about yourself and songwriting. You will create a clean path forward toward success in congregational songwriting.

I am not talking about success as the world defines it. You now have a clear plot of land on which to build a solid spiritual base for your psyche. On this land, you can build a songwriting ministry modeled on Holy Spirit values. Values that are critical as you plan how and why you write. These values not only make you a better person, they become a part of your spiritual attitude. They become the runway on which you start your flight to pursue God's call.

> *I am not talking about success as the world defines it. You now have a clear plot of land on which to build a solid spiritual base for your psyche.*

I call these values *The Ways of the Holistic Songwriter*. It will help you prepare *as well as propel and inform* your songwriting career for God. Whether you are young or old, an experienced writer or not, these ways of spiritual development define the career of the congregational songwriter.

After aligning your songwriting ministry with Jesus by understanding the concept of Fishing in Church, *The Ways of the Holistic Songwriter* is the first set of personal steps for you to take on the road of my songwriting blueprint.

THE 5 DISCIPLINES OF THE HOLISTIC SONGWRITER

As you read about Fishing in Church in Chapter 2, the promise from Jesus to his disciples that he will make them fishers of people can also fuel the congregational songwriter. Just as his disciples were charged with making fishers of people in his day, we songwriters are called to do so today. Our mission field is the church, where people of all faith levels come to learn more about Jesus.

In like manner, we are also charged by Jesus to be his disciples for such a time as this, for such a calling as this. We recognize *The Ways of the Holistic Songwriter* to be our disciple responsibilities—our disciplines.

We recognize The Ways of the Holistic Songwriter to be our disciple responsibilities— our disciplines.

1) *Take action* to align your songwriting ministry with Jesus.

Understand what it means to say yes to God and incorporate your individual faith into action. Your goal is to Make Jesus Famous; you can do this when you are able to dampen excessive individual pride and funnel that energy into listener-centric songwriting. It includes understanding that to be called to write songs for church is a higher calling, to show people through song how to connect their story with the true intention of God, and how to be a thought leader and lead worshiper who leads folks to the foot of the cross in their songs.

2) Commit to being biblically accurate in your lyrics.

Now, this is a big topic. What I don't intend is to give the impression that biblical accuracy depends on deifying the book itself. What I mean is to be scripturally precise, dedicating yourself to its study, and the faithful pursuit of Truth when writing about the story of God. Move your own biases out of the way. My definition of being scripturally accurate is to not lead people astray from the central message of Jesus in his Sermon on the Mount.

3) Discover 1:1 Songwriting Time with God

Listeners recognize authenticity like you recognize the smell of freshly baked bread.

This discipline has two wonderful byproducts. The first is that you strengthen your relationship with God as you commune with him daily with your songwriting. The second is that this experience will richly inform your songwriting and intensify your authenticity with your listeners. *Listeners recognize authenticity like you recognize the smell of freshly baked bread.* Your songs will rise above the pack because of this one area. The passion that comes from this exercise is your real advantage as a songwriter.

How can you accomplish this? Several ways. One is to do an exercise called Psalming that I learned through a songwriter mentorship from Dove Award nominee Krissy Nordhoff. Open the book of Psalms, any Psalm. Start accompanying yourself with your piano, guitar, mandolin, or banjo as you begin to sing the Psalm. This practice can inspire you, as you underline words and phrases while creating new songs, or just as you revel in your time with the Lord.

The practice of spending time with God in song is as old as the hand-printed word. The best example ever? King David, the author of the majority of the Psalms. All these works were born from his personal relationship with God, his angst with and his praise of God.

Many of his songs in the book of Psalms contain:

a. *His questions* or how he wrestles with God or his enemy.

> b.   How *he pleads* with God to hear him, or he outlines his enemy's failings.
>
> c.   He always returns to praise and worship or how God has the solution.

Each psalm dwells on one or more of these areas. It is a great formula for a song born from his heart of worship. This is the sound foundation of a writer who hears the voice of God. It paves the road in the development of good congregational songwriting techniques. It is the cornerstone on which we can build our house of song.

4) Learn to *express* your relationship with God.

It is how we press into our personal relationships with God, how we reach inward to discover more about his effect on our lives, and then turn those thoughts into lyrics. As we learn to express our relationship with God and share our experiences, we will become better writers because our listeners will relate.

We do this when we take the time with creative exercises as we prepare to write. Our inspiration can come from object writing lessons, the Bible, song idea diagrams, or personal journals.

5) Become worship leaders and volunteers.

You may be asked to come and lead worship. The pastor may know nothing about music and want you to select it for the worship service. You might have the opportunity to play an original song.

Small churches thrive on volunteerism. The pastors and the congregation love the excitement of someone who wants to serve because of the love in their hearts for God and people. They don't care if you are the best singer, musician, or the best anything. They see the beauty of your willing heart.

> *They don't care if you are the best singer, musician, or the best anything. They see the beauty of your willing heart.*

For such a time as this, you have been called to lead others in worship of the Most High God. The importance of open communication with the pastor in planning the service, including your capabilities and limitations, cannot be overstated. The more you and the pastor cultivate a great relationship and show that you are a team, the stronger the time of worship will be.

Select songs that support the pastor's message and support his or her comfort with you. Be a part of the church's worship team. Select songs that the people know and you are confident will lead them to the foot of the cross of Jesus.

Who knows? Maybe the pastor will be open to your singing a song that you wrote.

SUMMARY

These many topics are the subject of workshops in the faith-based songwriting community that you will read about in Chapter 6. They are also part of the curriculum of the Songs4God.net Worship Songwriting Academy that you will read about in Chapter 9. Each topic and sub-topic are covered in more detail in the online songwriting academy course. I encourage you to make these topics your own and include them when you start a faith-based songwriting organization.

For more detail on these subjects, see the second book in this series, *The 5 Steps to Get Your Songs Heard,* and *Fishing in Church,* the fourth in this series, at https://getyoursongsheard.com or https://books2read.com/stephenrobertcass.

5

The Songwriting Tools of the Proverbs 27.17 Small-Church Congregational Songwriting Revolution

"Songwriters write songs, but they really belong to the listener."

—Jimmy Buffett

BE ENCOURAGED. NO MATTER YOUR SKILL LEVEL, you can become a passionate and enlightened songwriter for the church. I will introduce specific songwriting tools and subjects that will help you become a dedicated congregational songwriter. These areas separate the Christian worship song genre from other genres and give the congregational song construction its style. Bring other songwriting skills, yes. But gauge them against this baseline list of essentials.

Your spiritual preparedness and exercises, your personal relationship with God, and the outflow from the *5 Disciplines of the Holistic Songwriter* inform the practice and enhance the effectiveness of these tools. Here is the short list:

- The song is everything
- Know the heart of worship
- The power of 1:1 songwriting time with God
- See the connection between theology and worship and songwriting
- Prosody and songwriting (prosody begins with the lyric)
- *The Proverbs 27.17 Lyric Formula*
- *The Proverbs 27.17 Melody Shape Tool*
- *The Proverbs 27.17 Song Critique Method* (includes rewriting a lyric for the listener)
- Kingdom Co-writing
- Share and build on public domain songs

THE SONG IS EVERYTHING

Eddie DeGarmo, well-known Christian songwriter, artist, and record company executive, writes that he and other executives sign artists according to how they rate in three basic areas: songwriting, musical instrument (or voice) skills, and charisma. Sure, they have other criteria. But these are the Big Three.

The triple threat rating was a short list of what people expected to hear. If an artist didn't have a songwriting strength, the record company or artists found powerful songs to showcase the other areas.

Except for the rare prodigy, most artists don't have this triple threat. But they shine in at least one of those areas.

Some examples: Bob Dylan is a brilliant songwriter but doesn't have a gift in the other areas. Elvis Presley had loads of charisma and his voice was unique and special, but not necessarily great, and he was never known as a songwriter. Kenny G is only known as a gifted instrumentalist.

> *Church songs are no different. People identify what we like to see, hear, and feel when we encounter a song. Talented singers and musicians are only a part of the equation.*

Church songs are no different. People identify what we like to see, hear, and feel when we encounter a song. Talented singers and musicians are only a part of the equation.

The Key to the Triple Threat

When we hear a song, we all know instinctually whether we like it. We are often quick to give our opinion, as well. If we hear a love song on the radio, it is memorable and singable if it tells a good story. In church, we hear a worship song and judge how it moves our hearts about God. We are touched by wonderful lyric and melodic skill when it masterfully tells some aspect about *The Greatest Story Ever Told*.

> *The song is everything.*

The song is everything.

Excellent songwriting in worship is the key to the triple threat. The songwriter is the catalyst that connects people with a great song. Without a great song, instrumental prowess and charisma don't have a platform to move our hearts.

> *Excellent songwriting in worship is the key to the triple threat.*

The Importance of the Congregational Songwriter

No other group of people on earth more deeply appreciate a well-written song, so rich with awesome theology, than folks attending a worship service. This audience expects a finely tuned message. The profound emotions generated and the strong imagery created by a well-constructed song can prepare our hearts to commune with God. People of faith and those searching can sense the depth of his unconditional love.

This is the tightest niche and most appropriate group of people for our best songs. When we write, we address the emotions and critical thinking of these people about the greatness of the Living God. The movement of the Holy Spirit in our hearts and minds amplifies the experience.

There is a special place in music for the congregational songwriter. People want to be ministered to and sing fresh songs about God's glory in Jesus Christ. The call of Christ magnifies the importance of delivering the clear and powerful message of the Good News.

And YOU, dear songwriter, are the contributor God has chosen for this work.

So be a listener and a contributor. As a listener, consider how the songs you hear affect you and those around you. Feel how they reach and inspire you. *In church, people know what moves them: songs about the Greatest Story Ever Told. This same story is — by far — the most written and talked-about story in the history of the world. This is the message that Jesus told us would change our lives forever. It is the most desired and sought-after message of all time.*

And YOU, dear songwriter, are the contributor God has chosen for this work.

We know that the song means everything to us because it communicates—it resonates in us—through stories, common emotions, similes, and metaphors.

Begin identifying yourself as a person with in-depth knowledge of the power of the song and how that can relate to successful congregational songwriting.

KNOW THE HEART OF WORSHIP

It is a lifelong calling for church musicians and worship leaders to learn to lead with the heart of a servant. There are many side streets, typical as we all work out our salvation, but worship team members are on a mission. Songwriters need to feed church musicians and worship leaders with servant-heart songs. Why? Because the primary job of a worship leader is to provide songs that point their people to the foot of the cross. You just can't take this job lightly if you want to see progress in winning hearts for God.

Jesus showed how we point each other towards humility by washing the feet of his disciples, then telling them to do that for each other. When we come to the foot of the cross, Jesus invites us to love the Lord God with all our heart, mind, soul, and strength while we love and care for our neighbor *with the same respect that we love and care for our self.* We are called to engage in an amazing balancing act. In essence—my words and not scripture—God says to us, "If you seek my face and love me and want to do what I desire, you will show the highest amount of mercy and dignity towards those around you."

Or as Micah 6:8 says:

*He has shown you, o mortal, what is good. And what does the Lord require of you? To **act justly**, to **love mercy**, and to **walk humbly with your God**.*

I created a blog post and a picture of the balancing act at https://worship-in-spirit-and-truth.com/the-balancing-act.

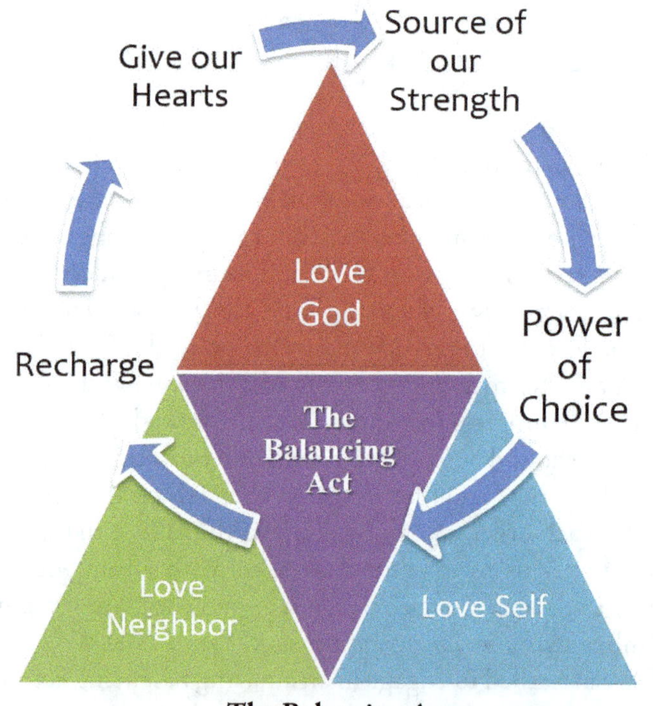

The Balancing Act

Worship leaders and worship team members struggle in life and fight the same battles as everyone else. They need God's mercy as they strive to serve his people. As a worship leader myself, I must tell you that this task of helping others on a worship team manage the balancing act is not easy. It is not because it is a job of micro-managing people; it is because we aim to present unity and remove distractions from the platform.

Worship leaders and teams are called to show the light of Jesus to a searching soul. They need to be on point with this and aligned with the pastor's message. Not that our human frailties won't seep through at times when we are on the platform; but, like the lead pastor, the worship leader and team need to bring their *worship and music A game.*

A good example of this point is a story I heard from Matt Redman, worship leader and songwriter. Speaking at a worship leader conference, Matt shared that he and his worship team were dismissed for a season by his lead pastor because the pastor didn't believe that Matt and the team had a primary interest in leading the people to the foot of the cross. He believed they had become distracted and more interested in being a good band.

> *Worship leaders and teams need servant-heart songs that remind us to wash the feet of each other, to pay attention to our self-care, and to tell God how great we believe he is.*

They eventually began playing in worship again at his church, but that episode inspired Matt to write a song titled *The Heart of Worship:*

> *I'm coming back to the heart of worship and it's*
> *All about you, it's all about you, Jesus. I'm sorry,*
> *Lord, for the thing I've made it, 'cause it's*
> *All about you, it's all about you, Jesus.*

Worship leaders and teams need servant-heart songs that remind us to wash the feet of each other, to pay attention to our self-care, and to tell God how great we believe he is.

We need to thank him in song for all the mercy he shows us and to tell him that we hear his call on our hearts. We need to thank him for his wisdom, and to tell him that we understand his justice is about showing mercy to the less fortunate.

The congregational songwriter recognizes this need. We understand that worship leaders are hungry for fresh songs that share the Good News of Jesus. And because we know that the song means everything to us, it needs to be on-point to communicate the will and the story of God. When the song is communicated well through stories, common emotions, similes, and metaphors, it not only resonates with us but with the entire congregation.

> *We need songs from the grass roots, songs that find its stories from inside church communities.*

We need songs from the grassroots, songs that find their stories from inside church communities. The congregational songwriter writes songs from their personal experiences and those of their local church family. Our songs need to be rooted in the heart of worship. Pour your lyric and song writing efforts into Jesus and his ministry to people.

THE POWER OF 1:1 SONGWRITING TIME WITH GOD

You read in Chapter 4, *The Ways of the Holistic Songwriter*, about discovering your songwriting time with God. Now, we will spend time developing that practice.

Spending personal time with God to enhance your relationship and your writing is crucial to foster the *desire* to supply servant-heart songs. This alone makes the worship songwriter unique compared to writers in other genres and is critical to finding and developing a heart of worship. *The real advantage is the power of the passion between you and God,* and how you develop your songwriting as your relationship matures.

Aligning our heart with God's will opens a beautiful pipeline of purpose in our Christian walk. It starts as we communicate with God daily. Some of us journal our thoughts as we hear him speak to us, whether it is during our prayer time or through people and situations. This is how we learn to translate the passion in our relationship into our songwriting.

> *Aligning your heart with God's will opens a beautiful pipeline of purpose in your Christian walk.*

Writing songs becomes an authentic journal of how we wrestle with and adore God (remember, listeners are absolutely attracted to authenticity). It is how we learn to write God's truths and our growth experiences in a way that listeners can relate to and value.

And a repeat of the example from King David, who did exactly this. Now we have a book of 150 of his, and his compatriot's, songs, *Psalms.* Here is Psalm 13:

For the director of music. A psalm of David.

How long, Lord? Will you forget me forever?
How long will you hide your face from me?
How long must I wrestle with my thoughts
and day after day have sorrow in my heart?
How long will my enemy triumph over me?
Look on me and answer, Lord my God.
Give light to my eyes, or I will sleep in death,

and my enemy will say, "I have overcome him,"
and my foes will rejoice when I fall.
But I trust in your unfailing love;
my heart rejoices in your salvation.
I will sing the Lord's praise,
for he has been good to me.

Many of David's songs in the book of Psalms contain:

a. *His questions,* or how he wrestles with God or his enemy;
b. How *he pleads* with God to hear him, or he outlines his enemy's failings;
c. He always returns to praise and worship, or how God has the solution.

Each psalm dwells on one or more of these areas. It is born out of his heart of worship, which was developed through his relationship with God. This method paves a road for the development of good congregational songwriting techniques.

King David knew that the song meant everything to him as a conduit to communicate and share his emotional experiences. (No, record company executives didn't invent the need for this passion, but they do a great job of recognizing.) Now it is our job as congregational songwriters to use these powerful tools to help tell the story of God.

Author Note: *David is the author of the majority of the Psalms. Some of the psalms were written by Asaph, the sons of Korah and other worship leaders and Songs of Ascents to the temple and to mark other occasions/events.*

SEE THE CONNECTION BETWEEN THEOLOGY AND WORSHIP AND SONGWRITING

"I think that the biggest failure of songwriting textbooks is not so much on technique, but more on the function of songs and in the community. **The biggest lack of understanding is the connection between theology and worship and music."**

Dr. Chuck Fromm, Lifetime Achievement Award by the Gospel Music Association in 1990, and founder of Worship Leader Magazine in 1992 Quoted from *An Analysis of the Need for a Congregational Songwriting Manual for the Evangelical Community*, page 64, by Travis Doucette https://digitalcommons. liberty.edu/cgi/viewcontent. cgi?article=1896&context=doctoral (emphases are mine)

The quote above from Dr. Fromm is exactly why I am writing this series of books and creating the Songs4God.net Worship Songwriting Academy. It is the connection between theology and worship and music. But beyond the concept of *why*, I need you to see I am not trying to reinvent the wheel about good and basic song education. There is literally a ton

> *What I am doing is inventing the wheel of the connection between theology and worship and music. I don't know if that has been done.*

of written material on writing songs. What I *am* doing is inventing the wheel of the *connection* between theology and worship and music. I don't know if that has been done.

So, I want to move next to *how* they are connected. There *is* specific songcraft education relating to congregational songwriting that I will show. But first, try to visualize the connection between great songwriting skills and local song theology as a *marriage. Like a marriage, the best result is when the two become one.*

> *The difference between our genre and any other is how applicable storytelling and relational language skills connect with the heart of worship.*

The difference between our genre and any other is how meaningful storytelling and relational language skills *connect* with the heart of worship. This happens in no other genre. Sure, there is a heart connection in great lyric writing of any type, but not the heart connection with the power of the Holy Spirit and God's ability to move among his people.

And in our songs, content is literally King. Our lyrics are paramount; they convey the story of Jesus. The world is hungry to hear theological truths, and this medium may be the most effective way to reach the masses. Add the unique skill set of *The Ways of the Holistic Songwriter* into the connection, and we have a truly exclusive skill set for the congregational songwriter.

Writing Songs for Your Audience

In many ways, congregational songwriting is like other genres, where all the great and rudimentary crafting tools apply. We use similar writing techniques, like creating word pictures or drawing to our senses using similes, such as, "like the fragrance after the rain." Or the use of anaphora, the repetition of a word or phrase at the beginning of successive phrases, such as, "all my heart, all my soul, all my strength." But notably absent are the "cute" trick phrases, such as the consonance, "nobility has the ability for reciprocity" or wordplay such as, "Central Perk." We use many of the same literary devices, but not those that draw attention to themselves.

Knowing about the connection and steering clear of lyric devices that draw attention to themselves shines a brighter light on discerning what works in congregational songwriting. What does work? Always remembering to write for your audience and that songs are stories. That's what works.

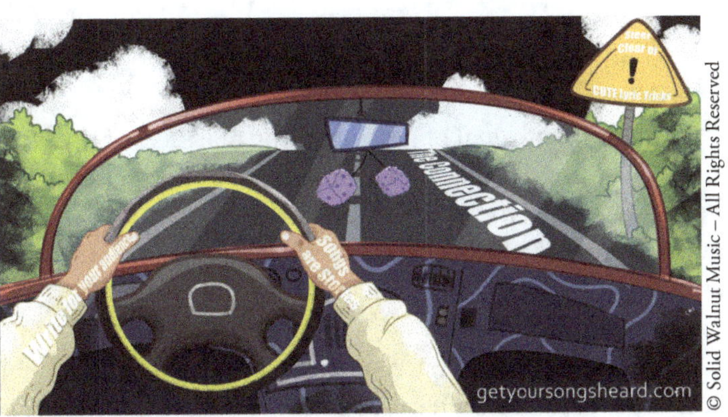

© Solid Walnut Music – All Rights Reserved

The worship songwriting car

PROSODY AND SONGWRITING
(PROSODY BEGINS WITH THE LYRIC)

Prosody defines the rhythm, stress, and intonation of speech. The definition of prosody — whether in poetry, speech, reading, or music — implies that songs communicate best when there is a lyrical synergy between all parts.

The synergy between all parts begins with the construction of the lyric. Seek to harmonize the emotional and imagery components of the story so it comes alive for the listener. Use:

- Common emotions, images;
- Empathy;
- Show, don't tell;
- Word pictures and details;
- Similes and personal comparisons.

Continually visit these tools to write about the emotions of your song.

The ultimate goal of prosody is the marriage of the lyric and the music. Keep the lyric conversational. The music helps to convey the same emotional message of the lyric, but that smooth flow depends on the natural and seemingly effortless story telling of the One Idea (central idea) and the main emotion.

As you build prose that reflects natural and conversational language, you create a natural pathway for the melody. You will tweak the melody so it reflects the emotional tone of the language and story, and the supporting music will amplify and connect even more deeply with the kernel of the idea for your lyric.

When you tell your story in a way that engages the listener with every word and every line, you've got something. Your songs will stand far above others.

Common Emotion and Images

Superb storytellers use a mechanism that brings their musings close to our hearts. It causes us to create scenes in our mind's eye. This internal scenery is one reason humans have been able to communicate so well over the eons.

A great song is never about you. Even if you are the subject, you write to engage the listener. Think about this: Great storytellers hook you in by sharing the emotions of their adventure. You are drawn into the story to feel their passion, intensity, confusion or doubt (whatever sentiment they are conveying) about their experience, their conflicts, and resolutions.

You can write a story about you or Jesus. But the listener will connect with and react to the common emotion and images you convey with your idea or story.

For example, the nails driven through the hands and feet of Jesus caused unimaginable pain to him. The word *unimaginable* creates a common image in our minds about that gruesome detail. You can describe that common image in a lyric and express in other terms what it is like.

> Led away to die, to be murdered on a tree
> To watch his trail of blood, to hear his
> painful screams
> To feel the hammer pound, see the anguish
> on his face

I cannot bear the scene, yet I cannot
turn away
He took my nails and I will ever glorify
his name

He Took My Nails
© 2023 Stephen Robert Cass

Empathy and Show, Don't Tell

As you construct a story using word pictures, comparisons, and common emotions, remember your job as a writer is to help manage the listener's expectations. You do this by using two tools:

- Empathy
- Show, don't tell

Weave the kernel emotion, or emotions, throughout the story or the lyric. Guide the listener through a journey of emotions. This is so effective.

Jesus, Jesus, Jesus, Your face is in my mind
Vivid, lasting, present, like a sunset-colored sky;
Jesus, Jesus, Jesus, come heal my broken heart
Draw me close with your everlasting arms,
And let me see You when I close my eyes.

When I Close My Eyes
© 2022 Stephen Robert Cass

I set the stage by repeating the name of Jesus to let the listener know I am praying and meditating on the experience of Jesus. Do you see how I grabbed her attention by inciting an image in her mind in the first line *plus* painting a picture of what that might look like in the second line? I compared the mental picture to a common beautiful and familiar scene: a sunset. If you are like me, you have experienced peace and calmness when you've witnessed a beautiful sunset. The similes and hooks are complete as they invite the listener into the story. *Can't you feel that peace when you see the brightly colored sky, too?*

I close the verse by telling Jesus that I long to think of him when I remember this picture. Now the listener possesses this memory and picture, too.

Going forward, let every lyrical decision relate to the underlying message of the story by writing a comparison of what it is like, a simile. This is how listeners remember stories.

No Story, No Song

No matter what type of song, it is *always* about a story, or a part of a story. It might not be a story song, but there is a story that shaped—or is shaping—the main idea kernel.

For some reason, we are built to tell each other stories. In worship songwriting, we get to write about the Greatest Story Ever Told and how that story has shaped our thoughts, and how it is shaping our world. With the deeper story of how we grow in our relationship with Jesus, how he affects our lives today, and how we respond to him, we have a ton of great story material.

One of the true secrets of telling a story and writing a great song is relating conflict and resolution—tension and release. We crave these details and want to hear how others handle life's challenges and how they resolve a situation.

The conflict can be of God's pure love contrasted with the evil one, or about the barrier to him, or of achieving our goal. Another is the conflict between God's greatness and our selfish desires. Folks are anxious to hear answers about how you handle conflict and receive inspiration about how they can handle their own.

Example:

> This is how I shake the darkness
> And break the hefty chains
> I call the Prince of Power
> The unmatched name of names
> Jesus, Jesus
> **The Unmatched Name of Names**
> **© 2019 Stephen Robert Cass**

You write because the story of Jesus causes you to write.

God is always part of the story whether he is acknowledged or not, a part of the action, being sung to or is the One singing.

As you relate the powerful central idea and tell how you are solving the tension, get your audience to pull for the narrator who is proclaiming God's story. Get the listener to participate in the writer's joy and cause them to sing!

The So What Test

There is more to lyric construction than just adding supporting words and thoughts. You should ask yourself this question at the end of every word and every line of your lyric: *So what?*

Meaning, how does what you just wrote relate to the kernel idea of your song? Use the *so what* test after every line. Think *build the story and ask "**so what?**"*. If the answer to "so what?" doesn't enhance the purpose of the lyric, it should be worked until it does. If it is fluff, delete it and start over.

Statements vs. Adding Action and Movement

If you only write statements when you are building the story, you will lose the listener in about five seconds. Add word pictures, details, action, and movement. Pulling from the *seven* senses of sight, smell, hearing, touch, taste, organic, and kinesthetic (read more about organic and kinesthetic in the next section), describe what you mean. Say it in a different or an unexpected way.

Think *conversational* and describe the scene.

Read the difference in the following example. The premise here is you have no food and you are hungry:

> The cupboard was bare
> I went to the store
> I ran back home

See how better it reads with details:

> The creak of the cupboard door echoed
> I ran like Santa Ana winds to the market
> My quarry in the bag, I quickly skipped home

Or in this example, the premise is that my Savior sacrificed his life for my sake:

> Jesus died for me
> No more pain
> I can live again

Your story can come to life if you add action and images:

> I nailed my shame to a tree
> The love of Jesus ran red
> Every breath is victory

© 2019 Steve Cass

How are you describing and solving the tension in the lyric you're working on now?

> **Pro tip**: the best songs describe the tension in
> the verses and save the release for the chorus.

Recap

Here is a quick summary of the tools used when thinking about how prosody begins with the lyric:

- Common emotions and images
- Word pictures and details
- Similes and personal comparisons
- Empathy
- Show, don't tell

And here is how to shape your ideas:

- Remember, if you don't have a story, you don't have a song.

- Use the *so what* test to assure that every line relates to the central idea.
- Add actions and movement.
- Pull from the seven senses.

THE PROVERBS 27.17 LYRIC FORMULA

Now that you have a method to shape your main idea, I want to share a custom tool that is essential to nurturing this seedling so you can create a full song. The following is a lyric writing system. It is not a template; it is a brief reference so you can create a solid structure and gather even more tools to serve the song, allowing you to create the best song from your main idea.

"In advertising, you have this small window to say the most you can. That's what songwriting is. The difference is that you get to put leaves on the trees and color 'em in."

Garth Brooks

How can you be sure the song you write is a strong one? Can you guarantee it will stick in the memory of your listener? How can you get the listener to concentrate on the main idea? The answers are that the song is not about you; it is about your listener.

The answers are that the song is not about you, it is about your listener.

Not knowing how to hone or communicate a great idea is frustrating. You know your audience, so craft stories for them. The best way to start is to use a proven lyric writing system. This will help you go after unique phrases which define well verbalized songs that connect with the listener. Never tell yourself what you write isn't worthy. Just write and write and write. Remember, King David and other worship leaders of the temple probably wrote 10,000 psalms, but only landed 150 on their greatest hits.

Here is the *Proverbs 27.17 Lyric Formula*. You'll find an infographic of this at https://songs4god.net/the-proverbs-27-17-lyric-formula. There is a link on the page to download a PDF version you can print and place it on the wall or keep it in a songwriting binder.

DESIGN

The **overall architecture** of a great song has these key elements:

The Power of One Idea

- Other lyrical ideas you have for the song should support the main idea of it. Every line of the lyric should support the central action of the One Idea. All supporting lines are thoughts surrounding the One Idea.

Prosody Begins with the Lyric

- Remember, prosody defines the rhythm, stress, and intonation of speech. It implies that the main idea of the creative work is best communicated when there's a lyrical synergy among all parts.

A Story (No Story, No Song)

- No matter what type of song, it's *always* about a story. Or a part of a story. It might not be a story song, but there's a story that shaped—or is shaping—the main idea kernel.

PREPARE

Prepare by gathering the building blocks for your lyric.

Have either individual or collaborative sessions to mine the most important words and phrases associated with the One Idea. Gather ideas and phrases from:

- The Bible
- Your walk with Jesus
- Your experiences
- Sermons, blogs, word cloud, etc.
- Your inspiration library (public and private)
- Object writing sessions.
  - A term used by Pat Pattison in his book *Writing Better Lyrics*
  - An exercise on how to express an experience with our *seven* senses.
    - Taste, feel, touch, hear, see, organic, and kinesthetic.
      - Organic senses are those that come from our body, such as heartbeat and breathing.
      - Kinesthetic senses are your feelings in comparison with the world around

> us, such as dizziness and the wind in my face, etc.
>> ▪ Example: a tree. Describe everything about it in a two-minute session.

- Use the resources above and write all things sensory on the topic. How does it make you feel? Can you describe any other emotions that come from the One Idea? Are there any smells or tastes involved? Are there any elements of touch? Or sounds? Or color? Or feelings?
- Word cloud (writing and connecting related words and phrases on a single page)
  - Explore and connect associated thoughts, words, and emotions.

BUILD

Build the framework with your blocks by developing these **essential elements**:

Create a Memorable Title

- The title is the product. It conveys the central thought and is the nerve center of your story. It advertises the central idea and emotion.

Design the Payoff

- *The payoff* is described as the line or a phrase in the song that gives the listener ultimate clarity for your message. It's often your One Idea, your main idea.

Build the Schema

- The schema is setting the logical order of the story for a lyric. The listener needs this order so they don't pause and ultimately stop listening; they just follow your lead. It is giving them a heads up about the five W's (who, what, when, where, and why) so you can lay the rest of the lyric on this framework.

Develop the Plot

- Develop *how* you'll tell the story. This goes hand in hand with …

Progress to the Payoff

- Continue to build listener expectations in the plot development toward the payoff.

Choose a Song Form

- Sometimes done consciously, sometimes a secondary concern. More important than the form is developing the One Idea through a story. But keeping lyric form in mind can be a great tool/template to develop your schema and plot to tell your story.

TOOLS

Craft your song for the benefit of your listener using tools such as:

Exposition, Conflict, and Resolution

- This tool is a nice and neat template to build your story or song parts around. Using the template, you will expose the scene or your singer's point of view or surroundings and tell of the singer's problem or situation. Then you resolve the situation or move the scene forward with action.

Storyboarding

- This method allows you to develop the plot of your story by writing each line of the lyric, or basic story idea, on a 3x5 card. Note on the card what is happening with your song character, any of the seven senses involved, or description of the scene. Lay the cards out on the table or floor in order of your story.

Picture and Caption

- To develop visuals and sensory perception for the listener, create snapshot images of the scene from the perspective of the singer. Ask yourself: How is the story developing? What is going on with their perception? How can the singer best relate the story to the listener? Now write the scene.

A Strong Start

- It is good to give the listener a strong word picture or message about the main idea within the first line or two. But more than that, tell the listener about the schema; lay out the storyline or framework.

Rhyme

- Using rhyme in writing helps us to remember stories. But the fact is, writing rhyme for the sake of rhyme only works for limericks. Not songwriting (unless that is your thing). Rhyming is a memory tool, not a tool to look cute. It is such a powerful tool because it can tempt you to write trite rhymes that stray from the central idea of the song.

Word Economy

- Christian artist and songwriter Morgan Cryar calls word economy "word PSI (word pressure per square inch)." Give more meaning in fewer words. Pack a punch with as few words as possible.

Literary Devices

- Literary devices help the listener analyze and understand your words. Avoid those that draw attention to themselves, there are many from which to choose. These distract the listener and detract from the main idea of the song. Here is a solid resource: https://literarydevices.net/

Contrast

- Use contrast to keep the listener's interest in your song. Contrast is a tool for both lyrics and music. For example, if your verse uses short words and phrases, use longer phrases in the chorus. There are many possibilities to consider. Take a look at

https://lyricworkroom.com/song-anatomy-101/
how-contrast-makes-any-song-more-compelling/

I go into rich detail of this lyric formula in my book *Fishing in Church*.

The Proverbs 27.17 Lyric Formula Infographic

THE PROVERBS 27.17 MELODY SHAPE TOOL

Some writers just seem to have the knack for designing great melodies. Often, writers won't have ideas for them before working out a lyric. That is generally my writing style. If writing melodies is not your forte, it might be beneficial to team up with a skillful melody maker. Whether writing separately or with a partner or team, prosody of the melody will define how well it is in lockstep with the rhythm, stress, and intonation of the conversational lyric. Overall, does the melody fit the mood and enhance the story of the lyric?

A memorable melody is the secret sauce of telling your story. If you have a great melody and sharply focused lyric that complement each other and they cause people to sing, you've got something.

> *A memorable melody is the secret sauce of telling your story.*

When congregations sing well, that means the melodies are sticky. A great worship service is, in part, memorable when people look forward to coming again and again to sing about their faith.

As you create and tweak the melody, be conscious of the:

- Range—the note range and singability
- Shape—the visual structure
- Repetition—how certain elements repeat
- Rhythm—the prosody of the melody with the spoken cadence of the lyric. Does the melody follow and complement the natural speech? Also, does the underlying beat of the music complement or compete with the melody?
- Feel—the prosody of the melody with the lyric setting. Does this melody reflect the mood of the lyric?

I created *The Proverbs 27.17 Melody Shape Tool* to help you keep an eye on all these aspects of a worship song. It is a visual aid for those who perform song critiques. You can make comments on the range, shape, repetition, rhythm, and feel (and *The Cry*, the top note or set of notes).

Here's an example from the most popular song of the twentieth century (according to the 2001 joint survey by the National Endowment for the Arts and the Recording Industry Association of America), *Over the Rainbow,* https://www.youtube.com/watch?v=oW2QZ7KuaxA.

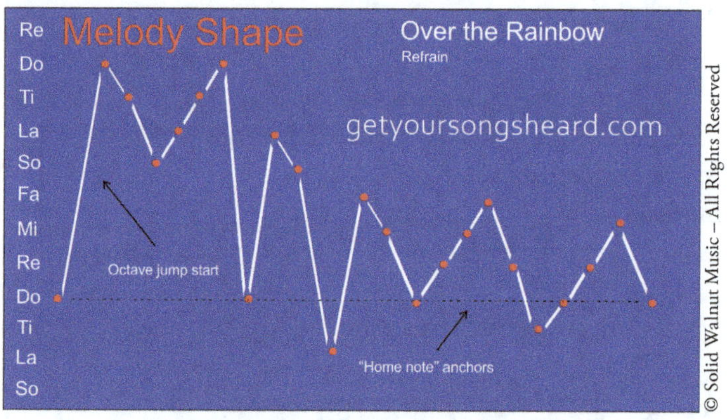

Over the Rainbow using The Proverbs 27.17 Melody Shape Tool

- Range—the note range and singability: *Probably singable, but most likely a song to enjoy performed by a talented singer*
- Shape—the visual structure: *A wonderful set of rise and fall patterns*
- Repetition—how certain elements repeat: *The melodic jumps and the symmetrical upward note patterns are mini-melodies*
- Rhythm—the prosody of the melody with the spoken cadence of the lyric. Does the melody follow and complement the natural speech? *Yes.* Also, does the underlying beat of the music

complement or compete with the melody? *This sort of tune has very little back beat.*

- Feel—the prosody of the melody with the lyric setting. Does this melody reflect the mood of the lyric? *Yes. The lyrics and melody are melancholy and replete with introspection and wondering, and full of hope.*

The "Cry", or top note, for *Over the Rainbow* is in the song's verse ("*…that's where you'll FIND me).*" But some consider the octave jump to start the song *The "Cry."* Think about the hopefulness you feel at the opening of this song. But I also discovered during research that the octave jump was a popular melody device used in songs from those days.

The song's prosody is the reason it was the most popular song from twentieth century. It is a complete story that conveys its message expertly and sticks in the mind of the listener.

Use this tool to analyze the songs you write as well as popular worship songs. Get great melody ideas from songs that work. Here is a popular worship song:

© Solid Walnut Music – All Rights Reserved

Great Are You Lord using The Proverbs 27.17 Melody Shape Tool

How would you answer the range, shape, repetition, rhythm, and feel questions for this song?

THE PROVERBS 27.17 SONG CRITIQUE METHOD

The only time you hear about song critiquing is when it is the result of a song contest. Thoughts of these contests conjure details that include condescending judgment. When I enter a song contest, I am convinced the judges have no idea what I'm going through—heart palpitations, clammy hands, disconcerting thoughts, why I am writing the song ... you get the picture.

But I have a better idea: Purposeful critiquing as a tool to make the song the best it can be; to create the art of the song critique.

You will learn about the Art of the Song Critique in my books and in the songwriting academy. It is an attitude adjustment on how to look at your song or your neighbor's song. It is a method of learning how to critique and to offer possible modifications to your songs according to the critique. This art is part learning how to strip away your ego so you don't take offense and part assimilating the advice you will receive about your song, so you improve it. Then, you resubmit it in order to continue getting advice to make your song the best it can be.

But the bottom line is that it is your song. It is up to you to decide on any of the advice. But you *do* need to listen and take the advice to heart on how to make your songs better, for your sake as a future strong congregational songwriter and for the sake of the future of your faith-based songwriting community.

During a songwriting contest, a panel of contest judges will focus on a handful of criteria, then rank the songs they feel best fit in the song genre of the competition. Ranking or rating a song is a distant consideration when using the Art of the Song Critique method with a panel of like-minded writers. Because the primary purpose of a *Proverbs 27.17 Song Critique Method* forum is to better the writer and the songwriting community, it can be used to help find the best songs to distribute to your local communities, or to decide on the best ones for a faith-based music publishing company to market to a wider audience.

The Proverbs 27.17 Song Critique Method, the Art of the Song Critique come to life in a form, is a survey. There will be any number of people involved who will critique the song and give their feedback to the songwriter through the creation of a report that includes their comments.

This is a next-level tool that I designed around the advantage of group learning. Crafted for the congregational writing style, it accelerates the learning curve and sharpens core writing skills. The model includes evaluating:

- Lyric writing;
- Melody creation;
- The prosody of the music, and;
- The viability for songs in the church environment.

You will evaluate your own songs and the creations of other dedicated songwriters. I base this evaluation and critique form on five critical song areas:

- Substance
- Structure
- Melody

- Prosody
- Viability

The following is only a sample of the questions and evaluations that you will drill down into the five critical areas:

SUBSTANCE

- Intended use of the song
- The power of One Idea
- The story aspect
- The central emotion
- Scriptural accuracy

STRUCTURE

- Strong start criteria
- Song form
- Rhyme
- Literary devices
- Sound repetition
- Memorable title
- Build to a payoff
- Word economy

MELODY

- Singability
- The range
- The repetition

- The rhythm with the spoken cadence
- The shape (visual structure)
- The feel
- The "Cry"

PROSODY

- First, do the lyric and melody belong together?
- Is the lyric conversational?
- Is the intended emotion conveyed throughout?
- Does the song make you want to sing it?

VIABILITY

- Can the chorus stand alone?
- Which ideas or images need expansion?
- Is the song easy to sing by the untrained masses?
- Would you characterize the song as congregational? What are your comments?
- Are the lyrics from the heart?
- Does the song have commercial value? Why?

The definition of congregational songwriting is found in the full version of *The Proverbs 27.17 Song Critique Method* questionnaire in my book *Fishing in Church*. It seeks extensive information about the song by asking follow-up questions to those on that list. You will find questions and criteria in addition to the above list. The PDF version of *The Proverbs 27.17 Song Critique Method* infographic seen below can be found at https://songs4god.net/wp-content/uploads/2022/02/Proverbs-27_17-Song-Critique-Method-Infographic.jpg

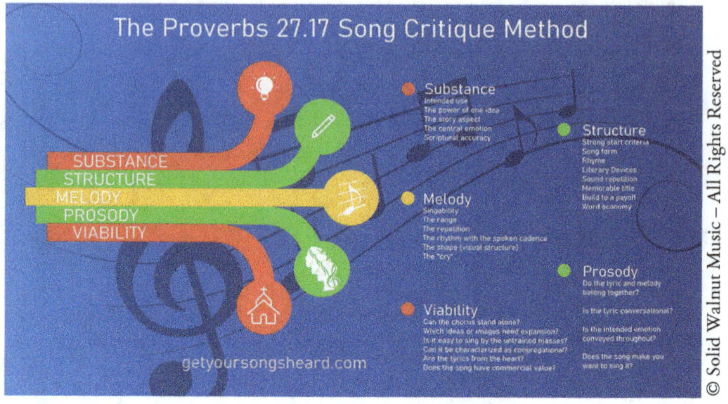

The Proverbs 27.17 Song Critique Method infographic

KINGDOM CO-WRITING

Your primary goal as a songwriter spreading the Gospel using *local song theology* is to serve your local community with heartfelt worship songs. So, serve the song first and make it worthy of the attention of your community. As I mentioned earlier in this chapter, the song is everything. Even the best songwriters in the industry figured out that the strongest songs come from collaboration. This is a staple in the modern country song world, and especially true in Christian music in the last several years.

Our reason for writing with each other is to serve the other writer with the best of our abilities, so our efforts are doubled, or even tripled. A co-written song takes the very best of the people in the room; it's a product of all, not input from one writer to help another complete their individual song. We have a common goal to serve our God and his people with our creations. Just as iron sharpens iron, we need each other to create the best songs possible.

Working together with another writer or two often flows naturally according to the personalities. It is not an exercise that must follow certain rules to affect a result. Your procedures might be different from what I am about to describe. But there are important things to know about the others before you begin, and ground rules that are important to ponder for the best results. We all learn by doing, so you can also use these tools in retrospect to deconstruct and reconstruct how you might do better the next time.

In Chapter 2, I introduced a tool that Krissy Nordhoff invented called the Songwriting Personality Test. Be sure also to take the extended version. It allows you to survey yourself so you know your songwriting strengths. You can purposefully seek writers who are gifted in other areas so you can present a stronger song.

Discover and explore these areas of your songwriting distinctiveness:

- Prophetic/Hearing
- Structure
- Content
- Melody
- Chords/Arranging
- Concept
- Producer/Track

Take the Songwriting Personality test and discover your strengths and weaknesses at https://krissynordhoff.com/test/.

There will be times when you write songs solo, then there will be times you will collaborate with another person or two ... or four. You will find that co-writing is totally different from your solo writing experience, and that it can sharpen your solo writing skills because of the special discipline required to create a song with others. You will find a new type of writing from the solo writing experience.

The bottom line is that all your efforts together are to serve the song, to write the best song possible. The attitude must be that you are all together to present your best effort. You will have a bad day and your co-writers might have to take up the slack, but you will also have constructive days when you are the one called upon to lead the others in the writing room (or the online portal). You all need to agree with that reality.

When you become a team, the decisions are driven by your unified purpose. When you co-write, you are all-in. All co-writers receive equal credit for the song, no matter the contribution. You agree that you will keep working on the song until all co-writers are satisfied with the product, and you all agree to share in any costs to demo the song.

There is a code of honor between songwriters. For the sake of your relationships, you agree you will not take the song to any other co-writers without the knowledge of the current co-writers. Like all good relationships, boundaries and rules should exist. You can honor this code together with a simple written agreement. As with all contracts, seek legal advice. Or not on this one. Just keep it simple.

Here are the *8 Rules for Kingdom Co-writing:*

1. Prepare
    a. Have a conversation or an email exchange in advance with your co-writers about any song-type or style expectations. For example:

    Is it a singable, congregational-style song or other? Specify the type. Is it a song for a special occasion such as a communion, Easter or Christmas, or call to worship?

b. Decide if you will bring ideas to the table, or if you will brainstorm ideas at your first meeting.

c. Have the discussion about what success looks like. Who is the target audience? What are the expectations for the song?

d. Unless it is already inked in the co-writing contract, talk about publishing administration for the song. Is the goal of the song to—someday—record and release it? Have you designated any one of you to have power of attorney, meaning all co-writers agree beforehand that the goal of the song is to be recorded, and one of you has the authority to give the legal permission for all of you to say it's ok for a record company to record?

2. Know Your Strengths and Weaknesses

a. You might be great at melodies but challenged when it comes to writing lyrics. Know going into your collaboration what is needed to bolster the other for success. Get to know the other songwriters beforehand to determine their strengths and weaknesses for a better match in the writing room.

3. Be on Time

a. Show your commitment to success by always being on time for appointments.

b. Be clear with all communication.

c. Be prompt and consistent with all things.

4. Find a Way to Say Yes
    a. "No" should not be used carelessly or callously. As a matter of fact, it is good to say *no* when establishing boundaries. You will find that during writing sessions, saying yes is more constructive than saying no. Make your *no* known in your co-writing agreement or in your initial conversations. In the session, temper your reactions with things like, "I'd rather …" or "Can we concentrate on …"
    b. Allow your time together co-writing to be fruitful toward the common goal of producing a memorable song. Find a way to agree—or at least be gracious—and let it be known that you will consider any possibility from your co-writers.
    c. You can let your individual assessments of your writing sessions determine the constructive conversations for your next session.

5. Be Patient
    a. Let discretion be the better part of your valor. We are all broken people trying to get our point across. Some of us do that with more grace than others.
    b. Allow people to fail and to say the wrong things. Give them a chance to come around to great mutual conclusions.

6. Encourage
    a. Some of you will have more writing experience than others. You will often find another writer can do a certain thing better than you, or they

know more than you. Listen to the stories from each other. Encourage each other to succeed, no matter how long you've been writing.

b. Our most creative moments come when we know we have the freedom to fail. Encourage team creativity by fostering an environment of support and mutual respect.

7. Be Honorable

a. Show your co-writers that you intend to produce an awesome, co-written song, not a solo effort with their input. If you discover that your co-writer is a slower thinker than you, be gracious. Your team is set to succeed together.

b. When hard times and disagreements come, remember your commitment to each other to see this project through to the end. If you decide to put it on the shelf for a time, so be it. Experience any failures and successes together.

8. Be the Co-writer Everyone Wants to Be With

a. No one is the perfect co-writer. Each of us will fall down at one of these points from time to time. But the mark of experience and maturity is when writers recognize their mistakes in a co-writing relationship and make amends.

b. The Golden Rule 2.0 applies well here, I think. "If you want others to want to be with you, you should want to be with them." Then show up.

If you strive to pay attention to these points, writers will call on you again and again to help produce winning songs.

SHARE AND BUILD ON PUBLIC DOMAIN SONGS

In another method of rewriting, Chris Tomlin and Louis Giglio used a public domain song and made a new copyrighted version. Here is more on how they took an amazing old hymn and made a beautiful new work.

The new title is *Amazing Grace (My Chains are Gone)*. Chris sang the original hymn much as it is known but made a few changes, including the addition of a powerful bridge.

Though the title itself is not copyrightable, it is still the banner for the new creation. He changed the banner to acknowledge the original work created by John Newton in 1772 and announced the new one by adding the parenthetical *My Chains are Gone*, the hook of the new song. Now, the underlying new work of words and music is copyrighted (music, lyrics, and music arrangement are the basis for the copyright). His record company copyrighted the sound recording. Both are now available so mechanical licenses can be issued.

Worship leader Tommy Walker has done this for several public domain hymns. One notable new creation is a version of the popular hymn *To God Be the Glory*. He added a bridge section and copyrighted the song in 2005.

You can do this, too, if you wish.

I have also done this by adding verses and choruses to old Christmas songs and hymns and have published them to CCLI.

The list of criteria used to determine whether a song is in the public domain is a little long. Generally, as of 2023, any song written prior to 1927 will be in the public domain and therefore available for anyone to perform, rewrite, or record. The use of any of them is free of royalties due to the owners of the song.

Check out https://www.pdinfo.com.

6

The Faith-based Songwriting Community

"As iron sharpens iron, so one person sharpens another."

—Proverbs 27:17

THE NEXT STEP IN THIS JOURNEY toward getting your songs heard is to join with a community of songwriters, administrators, and technical people who support your vision. You can take this step by joining forces with a handful of writers and begin your own small community.

> *And there is no doubt—we are better together.*

There is no doubt—we are better together.

What is the idea behind this faith-based songwriting community? It is the method by which you take your advanced knowledge of congregational songwriting and spread it to *your* world. Team up with other like-minded songwriters and make it happen. Start writing songs for your community with the idea that you and your community leadership will introduce the songs to your church.

You don't need to build a large organization, but you should continue reading this blueprint to see how this can be done and then modify it for your needs. Maybe you begin by joining forces with one or two other writers.

Developing a faith-based songwriting community begins with our individual connection with God and flows naturally among fellow congregational songwriters as we discover common goals. We can accomplish better songwriting by learning how to flourish together in co-writing and small songwriting groups.

The cornerstone of the songwriting community is the same principle of everything we do in the *small-church congregational songwriting revolution*. Proverbs 27:17 in the Bible. It drives everything that we want to accomplish. We can achieve more for the body of Christ *and* watch our individual songwriting skills grow to greater heights.

The local song theology solution, what I call The Proverbs 27.17 Small-Church Revolution, happens in two parts:

- Inviting songwriters called by God to seek congregational songwriting education; and,
- Building a symbiotic worship songwriting organization.

You can be sure: Even if your local church isn't listening to your songs, there will be plenty of others who will.

> *You can be sure: Even if your local church isn't listening to your songs, there will be plenty of others who will.*

"For where two or three are gathered in my name, there I am with them."
Jesus quoted in Matthew 18:20

Worship Songwriters

THE SMALL-CHURCH CONGREGATIONAL SONGWRITING REVOLUTION

My blueprint is a small-church local song theology solution for all songwriters, musicians, sound engineers, record producers, and song administrators of any size church.

What do I mean by "small church"? I briefly mentioned this in Chapter 2, *Five Solutions that Slay the Negatives.* The smaller churches may not be able to support a ministry that nurtures songwriters or songwriting communities to supply new worship songs. Church and worship leadership often don't have the time or resources.

The idea is to create fresh, relevant, grassroots songs that are written by you that are born from your view of how God is moving in your community. Worship songs provided by other churches and the music industry are uplifting, but your people need to hear your songs, too.

Why may small churches not have the opportunities to build a songwriting community? Mostly, because it takes dedicated personnel and resources to create or sustain this ministry … especially when the end goal is to distribute the songs. Unfortunately, but understandably, most churches don't have that sort of time or bandwidth.

Often when churches try to begin a songwriting community, the worship leader is the one who begins the effort, though their primary responsibility is creating a culture of worship in the church. Yet, even if the worship leader is in favor of this additional ministry, and the pastor and church leadership support and encourage it, it is unlikely to bear fruit unless it receives the attention and resources it deserves.

I would love to support my worship leaders if they tried to begin a songwriting community. But I know from experience that a worship leader's time is filled with song administration, creating an atmosphere of congregational worship and all the technical aspects involved with ensuring that everything works, guiding and mentoring team relationships, as well as fulfilling other staff responsibilities.

How can we make great songwriting part of every church? We invite the songwriters from within churches and create a songwriting organization *separate* from any church, separate from the obvious time and resources needed to sustain houses of worship.

The songwriters of the organization write songs from the experiences of their churches

> *If we intentionally nurture talented writers for the sake of the community, churches will thrive because of it.*

and communities. The songwriting organization feeds our churches with songs. If we design songwriting communities with the purpose of producing and promoting quality congregational songs, local song theology will thrive in the smaller and medium-size churches. If we intentionally nurture talented writers for the sake of the community, churches will thrive because of it.

RECIPROCAL RELATIONSHIPS

It is the organization that takes the lead to introduce the songs to worship and church leaders. The songwriter will not likely be asked to do any heavy promotional work. The songwriting organization becomes the voice and champion for the songwriters.

The organization reaches out to worship leaders and pastors.

The small-church local song theology solution is a plan for worship leaders and the songwriting organization to be the new gatekeepers for songs in local churches. Worship leaders are looking for fresh songs to introduce to their congregations, and it is my contention that they should not bear the burden of finding them alone. They are already busy. So, while they select songs for their worship services, the songwriting organization will make new songs available to them.

Worship leaders and pastors reach out to the organization.

Reciprocal relationships. Writers need good relationships with their local worship leader, but I'm referring to the relationship between the organization and worship leaders.

Many small churches have no worship leader. It would thrill pastors to know there is an organization that cares about delivering quality songs to them.

If a worship leader is also a songwriter, they might introduce some of their songs to their church. But it also means they may be open to finding songs from other songwriters that communicate the spirit of their congregation. Most would be very open to finding excellent songs from writers in their community, songs that align with the pastor's message and the heart of the church.

It will impress worship leaders that a dedicated congregational songwriting organization wants to help their cause. A worship leader myself, I often feel alone in the world and in way over my head. Sometimes, it seems as if there is no one to help. I imagine other worship leaders feel the same way from time to time. This is where the songwriting organization can step in and offer songs.

It will energize worship leaders when they understand how serious the songwriting organization is in their mission, and how dedicated they are to their first partnership (to be the champion for their songwriters). Worship leaders need to find fresh and pertinent songs, and the songwriting organization can supply them. The organization will be aware of the recent messages from the pastor, and happenings in

> *Worship leaders need to find fresh and pertinent songs, and we can serve them.*

their church community because of the first partnership with the songwriters.

Worship leaders are also managing other aspects of church and worship team dynamics. They certainly do not need more on their plates. Churches and worship leaders need a sympathetic songwriting organization that has a process in place to provide new songs, one that understands and addresses concerns church leaders have about the quality and availability of songs that meet the needs of the congregation, and one that anticipates concerns others may have about the organization. For example:

- Where is the heart of worship within the organization?
    - They may wonder: "Is that the true nature of the organization, or is there another agenda? How will they stay on point to serve my church?"
- Do they have a process to execute the organization's song service?
    - A published roadmap of what worship leaders can expect from the organization, namely:
        - Technical leadership and details, and to see plans of action in place. How does the organization:
            - select songs?
            - make songs available for worship leaders?
            - develop songwriters?
            - manage song publishing administration?
            - produce demos or other recording projects?

When we manage these questions, and advertise that we do, worship leaders will see how valuable the songwriting organization can be. Some worship leaders may not be ready to use the organization, but they need to be impressed by *our* complete readiness and how we present undeniably quality songs, songs worthy of their attention. Hopefully, they will see how this can take the pressure off them.

REACHING OUT TO SONGWRITERS

The partnership plans:

- A group of worship songwriters dedicated to learning congregational songwriting techniques
- An organization dedicated to support those songwriters in their congregational songwriting education and song promotion goals and dedicated to expanding local song theology
- Churches and worship leaders willing to partner with the organization

It all begins with reaching out to songwriters. Songwriters may or may not have any opportunity to contribute songs to their church. *But by joining the local song theology songwriting organization, they will find that they can have a voice in their community and an opportunity to share their works where before they had no avenue.* The number one job of the songwriting community is to get their songs heard by their local churches.

I want to encourage songwriters in churches to see the value of a more organized and dedicated songwriting community—*outside of any church*—to reach your worship leader and church leadership with quality worship songs.

THE INVITATION

I am excited to invite you to join or begin a Proverbs 27.17 Small-Church Revolution songwriting community based on local song theology.

If you are an experienced songwriter at *any* level and:

- Struggle with confidence and are not sure if you will pursue a solution,
- Think you will never be a strong enough writer to compete,
- Have no musical skills but a deep desire to learn,
- Not sure where to find song ideas,
- Can start songs but don't know how to finish them,
- Are afraid to show your songs for fear of rejection,
- Fear you will never become the songwriter you were designed to be,
- Are overwhelmed with where to begin,
- Have anxiety to get it done because you know this is the best way to express your gratitude to God,
- Are stuck in a loop, creating the same chords and melodies in your songs,
- Are looking for a solution to reignite passion for your songwriting,

- Have had success in the past, but want to take your craft to a higher level,
- Are a worship leader who writes songs, but so far, the songs have not received favorable responses,
- Are frustrated and have analysis paralysis,
- You know God designed you to write great songs, but you need direction,
- Know it's not about the money, it's about the message,
    - Sure, you want to get paid for your work, but spreading songs of inspiration and hope are more important,
- Feel like giving up because you are afraid to approach your worship leader:
    - You feel that your lack of experience or training will be apparent to your worship leader.
    - You need guidance, but don't want to take up the worship leader's time.
    - You know the worship leader often shares the same perceptions about songwriters and you wonder if they have the capacity to shepherd you.
- Feel that the only avenue you have is to approach the mainstream market, and you feel you'll never be up to that standard;

… then this songwriting community is for you. I invite you to take part and grow while you help others do the same.

THE SONGWRITING COMMUNITY BLUEPRINT

As Dr. Chuck Fromm personally encouraged me to begin a local song theology community—through my connection with him through Worship Leader Magazine workshops—I want to personally encourage you to build one.

Remember, the organization is separate from any church. But it must have a commitment-driven visionary in leadership, 100 percent dedicated to the success of the songwriters and the community. Is the songwriting community leader a worship pastor? Sounds good to me!

No matter the size or the vision, *the mission* for the organization remains:

- Help each other become the champion songwriters for their congregations.
    - Sharpen each other with continual worship songwriting activities: speakers, mentors, lyric and melody crafting exercises, song review boards, workshops on worship songwriting philosophy, co-writing, critiquing, advanced songwriting techniques, and learning how to share the songs with their worship leaders (The organization should take the responsibility of contacting worship leaders; however, everyone should always foster a great relationship with their local worship leader.)

The two principal methods to execute the organization's mission:

- The writers or the group identify their strongest songs.
    - They create simple demos and lead sheets in preparation to share the songs. Depending on which way group leadership wants to go, this could be as simple as sharing a few songs

between churches all the way to blossoming into a full-blown record label.

- The group or the writers register their songs with CCLI to prepare for multiple church use. Song administration is key to generating success.
  - No matter the size of your organization, this is a must, because CCLI SongSelect makes the songs available for local, regional, and national church audiences. Because of the association with CCLI, the organization generates revenue that can be used to fund future organizational causes; it will also be a great confidence booster.

Start with a small leadership team of maybe three people to help keep the focus on the mission and the methods. Having an odd number on the leadership team will help you stay on track and facilitate majority voting. Manage this list of top-level activities and functions:

- A regular leadership feedback meeting
- Meetings about time commitments and administration goal setting
- Songwriting meeting agenda topics
- Worship songwriting philosophy curriculum
- The Ways of the Holistic Songwriter
- Workshops about knowing the heart of worship
- The power of 1:1 songwriting time with God
- Realizing the connection between theology and worship and songwriting
- *The Proverbs 27.17 Lyric Formula*
- *The Proverbs 27.17 Melody Shape Tool*
- *The Proverbs 27.17 Song Critique Method* (and rewriting a lyric for the listener)

- The 8 Ground Rules for Kingdom Co-writing
- Share and build on public domain songs
- Lyric and melody crafting exercises
- Guest speakers or other activity
- Critiquing forum
- Open mic
- Breakout writing sessions
- Song promotion forum
    - Songs ready for promotion to churches
    - Songs selected for the next recording project
        - Maybe the recording function is in step with the faith-based music publishing company that you'll read about in the next chapter.

Again, if you're new and have no connections to get songs recorded, align with the right people. Start small. Act as if you will grow to the level of releasing recordings into the market.

Organization objectives and tasks:

- Record basic or full band demos
- Create lyric sheets and chord charts
    - Work toward these outcomes. Don't get overwhelmed and try to do it all yourself. Surround yourself with people who have this passion.
- Song marketing
- Organizational marketing
- Treasury
- Membership dues
- Royalty distribution (more descriptions in the next chapter)

- Song administration (more information coming in this chapter)
- Songwriter technical education (keep reading for more information)

SONG CRITIQUE FORUM

The lifeblood of this songwriting organization is the song critique forum. It follows the *Proverbs 27.17 Song Critique Method* found in the previous chapter. I cannot stress enough the critical value of creating an environment where songwriters can learn and grow to be better in their craft. The organization must embrace this mindset in order to educate the songwriter *and* ensure its own growth.

> *The lifeblood of this songwriting organization is the song critique forum.*

Weave song critique into the very fabric of the organization from the beginning. Bake this activity into the songwriter's group exercises. Embed the song critique system and philosophy so they become a critical function of the group at large. Encourage members to use the methodology as they critique their neighbor's song to help each other grow. Build an environment where they will learn the value of co-writing and collaborative relationships with other professionals.

At the very minimum, communicate to organization members the benefits of following an effective song critique forum that allows each writer to develop songwriting techniques and experience personal growth, not to mention songwriting community advancement. Emphasize how they will also witness the growth of their peers and the organization as they journey together and celebrate together when their best songs are released. Convey to them that an effective song critique forum will become part of the group DNA and it will be a regular activity of the organization.

I intentionally designed the song critique forum so songwriters, their writing partners, and the community excel at a rapid pace. Group learning inspires each member—each one challenges the other to grow. Iron sharpens iron.

Mastery of all the custom and next-level tools will amplify songwriting talents and results while fueling the engine of the songwriting community and its future publishing company.

You will find an in-depth view of the art of the song critique in my books *The 5 Steps to Get Your Songs Heard* and *Fishing in Church.*

PREPARE TO MARKET THE DEMOS

There can be long conversations about the best way to record and make your song demos. Now is the time to cultivate the relationships with the chord chart and recording gurus in your life (please invite them to become supporting members of this songwriting community!).

The next order of business for the songwriting organization is to register your songs with CCLI to prepare for multiple church use. This is more than placing songs in a marketplace; joining CCLI is a critical part of the plan to help individual songwriters and the organization make their songs available to local churches first, then to the wider world. Song administration and registration with CCLI is how to best prepare for success!

I don't work for CCLI, even though I keep mentioning it. I simply believe in the reason for its creation, its mission, and how we can use it to accomplish our own goals. Explore their website, www.ccli.com, and I think you will agree.

Registering your songs with CCLI is an absolute must for three reasons:

- You are advertising the need for church song license protection for churches.
- You are encouraging the church to adhere to the law and to help pay you for your work.
  - For an in-depth report on church song usage and legal obligations, see my special report *Worship Songs and the Law: How Churches Stay Legal and Songwriters Get Paid* and my book *Fishing in Church* (please visit https://getyoursongsheard.com for bulk quantity discounts or https://books2read.com/stephenrobertcass to see all places where the books are sold).
- By providing the CCLI song registration number, the church can report the usage of the song.
  - Auto-reporting of song use is a feature in CCLI, MultiTracks, Loop Community, and other worship song applications.
  - CCLI bases their decision on whether to make lead, lyric, chord charts and audio samples available in SongSelect by how many churches report the use of the song. They also recommend that you send them an email with the church information if you receive requests for your songs. They will document these requests.

- ○ When your songs reach CCLI coverage criteria, churches can download the CCLI version of the chord, lead, and lyric sheets.
- ○ Your song products will be available in the SongSelect catalog. Their chord charts and lyric sheets are adjustable by song key before you print them. This is perfect for the churches that request your songs, and your songs will be available for download by over 250,000 churches around the world.

GETTING OFF THE GROUND WITH MEMBERSHIP

Membership in your songwriting organization is to encourage ownership, accountability, and commitment for accomplishing the tasks at hand. Design engaging membership criteria that will motivate participation in setting and accomplishing the goals of the organization.

I recommend that you develop the criteria based on three levels of membership:

- Associate Member
  - ○ A writer or musician interested in the goals of the group. Until a writer understands your vision and the responsibilities of all members, I'd bring them on as an "associate" member.
- Writer Member
  - ○ A writer or musician who has signed a contractual agreement with the organization. They are committing to the overall goals (more

about what might be included in the contract in the next chapter).

- Support Member
  - A person who offers support to the organization—such as a musician dedicated to making chord charts or a recording studio engineer managing demo projects—and has asked about becoming a member but is not under a song contract.

Membership is an interesting conversation all by itself. You will arrange and rearrange this over time to find the right fit for what you are doing. The idea is to organize and define exactly each level of membership along with its responsibilities.

Membership can support your recording and song administration expenditures. Should you charge dues? That is your call. But consider that a person is more apt to be committed to what they invest in. You could start with $5 per month or $50 per year for an Associate Member, $10 per month or $100 per year for a Writer Member, and $5–50 per month for a Support Member. There should be a dedicated fund in place to cover demo and song preparation expenses, pay for top-quality guest speakers, and investment in song catalog management. You can prepare any sort of scheme to raise funds.

Membership dues isn't a profit idea. It is an incentive to sustain the goals.

Charging dues isn't a profit idea. It is an incentive to sustain the goals.

WHAT TO EXPECT

Don't let your lack of knowledge and experience scare you at this point. I encourage you to keep the community simple so you can focus on the music, serving local congregations, and getting your songs heard. But the songwriting community you have created will take you and like-minded people even further as you learn and grow together. It will amplify your efforts as a congregational songwriter.

The next chapter will dive into what drives the leadership of your songwriting community and provide a music publishing and record company building overview. Share this section of the book with like-minded songwriters who might have the organizational bug.

7

The Faith-based Music Publishing Company

The Champion of the Congregational Song and Songwriter

THE GOAL OF THIS GRASSROOTS music publishing organization is to ensure that the songwriting community flourishes in their mission to reach local churches. The organization will oversee all recording activity, distribution, legal compliance, and song administration. Its survival depends on the viability of the songwriting community.

Further, their only clients are the faith-based songwriting community and the songwriters. It will specialize in songwriter advocacy, and it will stand ready to promote their best songs to local communities and the wider world.

All in God's will and timing.

Let me assure you right now, however, you don't *have* to create this music publishing company to realize your congregational songwriting dreams. You can simply use the songwriting community and its continuing education to fulfill your task of becoming a sought-after songwriter and deliver songs to the local community. But you can expand your outreach to the community and the rest of the world by taking the next step and creating a song delivery machine: A faith-based music publishing company.

Expand your outreach to the community and the rest of the world by taking the next step and creating a song delivery machine: A faith-based music publishing company.

It could, depending on the arrangement with the songwriting community, take charge of the song distribution to local worship leaders and pastors. But it ideally remains in its own lane as an administrator, distributor, and promoter.

You, the songwriter, and you, the person supporting songwriting, have invested your heart, your time, and your brain power to learn how you can make this songwriting dream a reality. Joining with like-minded people in a songwriting community is the first and most critical step to getting your songs into hungry churches. This next step is also crucial because it amplifies the results of the songwriting community.

Joining with like-minded people in a songwriting community is the first crucial step to getting your songs into hungry churches.

Recording, developing, and delivering song demos might be the responsibility of someone in the songwriting community, but *how* all that gets done might also be accomplished by someone in your new publishing company.

The songwriting community and the publishing company must be symbiotic; that is, they need to function with the same mission, getting songs to local churches.

Some tasks of the publishing company will be:

> *The songwriting community and the publishing company must be symbiotic.*

- Recording and producing demos
- Creating lead and lyric sheets
- Marketing digital music and lead/lyric sheets
- CCLI/PRO (Performance Rights Organization) song administration
- Songwriter publishing agreements
- Songwriter management (These individuals advocate for the songwriter and help them navigate through any legal or other requirements)

Some of these functions could be done by either the songwriting community or the publishing company. Share responsibilities according to your plans and skills with the larger goal in mind: Spreading local song theology. Your company design is completely up to you. I'll provide the blueprint for the critical functions.

No matter who or how, here are the tasks that support that larger goal:

- Educate and nurture solid and sought-after songwriters,
- Write and deliver songs on how God is moving in your community and,
- Record and market the best songs to the wider world.

Distribution to your local church communities is always the priority.

GETTING ORGANIZED

The following descriptions contain important topics for songwriter educational opportunities. If you are interested in songwriting community and music publishing administration, take note to offer these in classes, webinars, discussions, and Q&A sessions.

For the songwriter reading this who is beginning to freak out because you don't want any part of the business side of songwriting, you should know two things:

- You and your co-writers don't *have* to create a songwriting community or music publishing company to become sought-after songwriters in this small-church congregational songwriting revolution.
- You should seek out other songwriters, recordists, audio producers—anyone interested in supporting your songwriting vision—to learn the ways of songwriting administration. It takes many hands and minds.

Please keep reading so you see how this works.

Songwriters, understand that the education for you that will come from the music publishing administrators includes specific topics and sub-topics for your benefit and continued growth:

- Where and how to register for royalty payments in 2023 and beyond
- Congregational songwriter priorities regarding royalties

- Why you should pursue an exact form of copyright
- Exactly where and how to have your songs copyrighted
- Copyright history as it pertains to the congregational songwriter
- Copyright law specific to congregational songwriting
- The rights of a songwriter
  - You own the publishing rights until you give them away
  - What is each right?
  - What can I do with each right?
- How public performance royalties work for your benefit
  - Specific to worship songwriters
- How songwriters benefit from church song licensing
- When churches are or are not exempt from US copyright law
- How a music publisher makes money
  - How a music publisher distributes money to you
- All about songwriting contracts with a faith-based music publisher

After all, the goal is to build a faith-based song publishing organization that is fully aligned with, and dedicated to, the mission of the songwriting organization. And the songwriting organization will be dedicated to the reputation and mission of the songwriter, whose greater mission is to write songs that honor and glorify the Lord and invite others to do the same.

There are no other goals for it except to amplify the success of the songwriter and songwriting organization by making and distributing grassroots recordings.

Consider this cycle that ends in victory for your songwriting team:

- You write or co-write a song.
- Have it critiqued by the forum.
- You and your co-writers improve the song based on feedback from the critique.
- You submit the song to the promotion committee and receive a positive review.
- Produce a demo of the song.
- Have all chord charts prepared for it.
- Songwriting organization leadership registers the song in all the right places.
- The organization promotes the song to churches and worship leaders.
- The faith-based music publisher promotes the song as a Spotify single, or
- Several of the recordings are added to a compilation.
- The publisher promotes and showcases your recorded music to regional and national bands and audiences.

NOW imagine scaling this model to promote ten or more songs simultaneously while promoting these recordings to regional and national Christian bands and artists. Imagine creating a showcase for these songs and hiring a top band to perform them. You invite the media, music industry executives, and local, regional, and national church leadership.

This is music to my ears as a songwriter. I hope this victorious vision can be yours, too.

SONG ADMINISTRATION, LEGAL, AND SONGWRITER MANAGEMENT

I won't get into lengthy descriptions of the nuts-and-bolts functions of the faith-based music publishing company here, but I will give you the bullet points of the plan. I dive more deeply into the philosophy of each point in the second book in the series, *The 5 Steps to Get Your Songs Heard.*

At the risk of being repetitive, know that the goals and functions of the songwriting community and music publishing company are ultimately the same: that of spreading local song theology. Envision their symbiotic nature, each performing their own unique tasks and roles yet working together to accomplish their common goals.

The following topics and sub-topics will be a part of the music publishing company plan and will be a part of the curriculum of the Songs4God.net Worship Songwriting Academy.

- The basics of the Hillsong music publishing model
  - What this model means and how we can adapt it to our own
- How the commitment to the songwriter drives this music publisher
- The duties and priorities of this faith-based music publisher
  - Compliance with copyright law
  - Moral commitment to the songwriter and community

- o The interpretation of music company practices according to its faith-based objectives and integrity
- The types of song contracts to be used
  - o The full implications of each type of contract
    - Legal obligation to copyright law
    - Moral commitment to the songwriter and community
    - Internal organizational integrity of contract compliance
  - o Why one certain type of contract *should* be used
- Possible revenue sources for the publishing company
  - o Income distribution plan
  - o Revenue sharing opportunities
- Master recording ownership and transfer schedule
- The faith-based music publisher song promotion plan

How can local songs possibly compete with those from the music industry? Because well-written, listener-focused, grass roots songs will be as desirable or better. Here is the story of how the influence of two well-written, meaningful, community-inspired songs awakened the heart of worship in many communities around the world.

> *How can local songs possibly compete with those from the music industry? Because well-written, listener-focused, grass roots songs will be as desirable or better.*

INSPIRATION FROM THE GRASS ROOTS

Dr. Tanya Riches spoke at the Worship Leader Magazine's songwriting conference I attended, hosted by Dr. Chuck Fromm, in 2013 in San Juan Capistrano, CA. Dr. Riches is a pastor, songwriter, administrator of Hillsong United, and master's program director at Hillsong College. But perhaps her greatest accomplishment was that she wrote a song during a trying time as a fifteen-year-old girl attending Hillsong Church. She related that time of her life to us:

> *"When I was fifteen, I wrote a song called Jesus What a Beautiful Name which ended up in the top ten CCLI songs in Australia and New Zealand. And one thing that I'm very passionate about is that song is connected to a very particular story in our church. It was the first song released after our worship pastor stood down following a moral failure. As a fifteen-year-old, it was quite huge for me to think about because this was the song that encouraged Hillsong Publishing to keep publishing songs ... There are sounds that are particular to places and there are moves of God. And we're trying to recreate them. The gospel and worship are universal, but sound is particular. Our job as worship songwriters is to find the sounds of your community ... it's really about them. It's about who they are. Worship with the sound from the grassroots."*

Hillsong released *Jesus What a Beautiful Name* in 1996 on their fifth live album, God is in the House. This was the first album released after Darlene Zschech became Tanya Riches' and Hillsong Church's new worship leader. With the explosion of Darlene's song in 1993, *Shout to the Lord*, and a later 1996 distribution deal with Integrity Music for the US market, Hillsong Music Publishing was soon to become an international phenomenon.

SHOUT TO THE LORD

There is a reason that the song *Shout to the Lord* remains one of the most popular worship songs in the world going on thirty years. Hillsong Church intentionally maintained a rich, focused basis of local song theology and aligning their local music with the message of the pastor. They made concrete decisions in those early days to define their local music ministry *(they prayed about and defined their calling)* and on how to publish their music for their ministry *(they took charge of writing their plan of success and next steps)*.

Yes, it is a skillful, life-changing song written by their worship leader, Darlene Zschech, but the world wouldn't know about that great song without the commitment from Hillsong Publishing to follow God where he was leading them. Their commitment and obedience led them to get their songs out into their community and to boldly forge ahead with their next steps to get them out to the world.

This same song visibility from CCLI will help propel your songwriting organization in this next stage of the small-church revolution.

The song ministry of Hillsong Church was purpose-driven: First to deliver new worship songs for their local community, then actively pursue nationwide, then worldwide distribution. CCLI, the best marketing tool ever created for the Christian songwriter, was a large part of their success from the standpoint of song visibility to other churches.

> *The songwriting organization has no obligation or concerns other than to deliver well written songs full of spiritual truths to the people of God.*

This same song visibility from CCLI will help propel *your* songwriting organization into this next stage of the small-church revolution.

IT'S NOT ABOUT THE SONGWRITING ORGANIZATION

Your faith-based songwriting organization, music publishing company, and your fellow congregational songwriters will flourish in part because of your association with CCLI.

This grassroots idea of a local song theology solution—the effort to join the small-church songwriting revolution—is not just to make recordings and create hit songs. Making records is fun, but that is not the focus. The songwriting organization has no obligation or concerns other than to deliver well written songs full of spiritual truths to the people of God. Local song theology

> *Local song theology songwriters exist to write songs that reflect how God is moving in our communities. Stay rooted in this mission.*

songwriters exist to write songs that reflect how God is moving in our communities. *Stay rooted in this mission.*

Faith-based songwriting communities and publishers can bring hope to those who are called to write songs for God so they can create songs that bring hope to others.

PREPARATION FOR INCOME SOURCES

The topic of *income from digital royalty sources* should be offered as continuing education for us all. Digital royalties and mechanical reproduction licensing are changing in the United States because of the Music Modernization Act of 2018. Read a better description of what this means for worship songwriting in my book *Worship Songs and the Law.* Please put this book on your reading list so you can have this knowledge and pass it along to other songwriters.

Frequently update writers in your songwriting group on how royalties work. Talk about upcoming changes in the copyright laws that might affect them. Make it a point to have presentations and discussions with all members about royalty income sources.

The bottom line is that all forms of royalties and fees in the music business should be a part of the member communication plan. All income distribution and revenue sharing are the prime responsibility of the organization.

Here is the larger view of possible income streams:

- Organization membership dues
- CCLI royalties—goes to the song rights holder of record

- Performance Rights Organization (PRO) *writer* income—goes straight to each writer (in the United States)
- PRO *publisher* income—goes straight to each writer, if they signed up with the PRO as a publisher *or* goes straight to the songwriting organization if the writer signs a publishing contract with them (in the United States)
- Physical and digital sales of recordings
- Song exploitation income (refer to my book *The 5 Steps to Get Your Songs Heard*)
- Print and digital sales of sheet music
  - Individual sheet music and folios (song collections or multiple pages)
- Mechanical reproduction licenses
  - Others who want to record your song pay a mechanical reproduction fee, song track licensing
- Synchronization licenses for film and TV
  - Broadcasters pay for the use of the underlying work
- Grand Rights
  - When your music is used on the drama stage
- Foreign Royalties
  - Royalties and usage fees collected outside your country
- Unforeseen collections
  - Income from exploitation not on this list, or from technology yet known

CCLI income from the full local song theology distribution effort is the most probable in the beginning. You should concentrate on CCLI income and administration, more than the other areas. But in the long term, be prepared for the other income sources.

I can't emphasize enough that it is not about the money from CCLI; the value is in the song distribution through them.

Mold your ideas for your music publishing organization around these basic income streams to determine how much attention and effort you will give each source of income.

There is detailed information about CCLI and PRO income sources in my books, *The 5 Steps Get Your Songs Heard* and *Worship Songs and the Law.*

8

The Small-church Manifesto Conclusion

"You got this!"

—Me

SLAY THE NEGATIVE MESSAGING that you were likely conditioned for and don't let that influence you. Pray where God would have you as a songwriter.

Where do you see your future as a songwriter? Join the small-church songwriting revolution. We are dedicated to nothing short of pure worship song output no matter the song style, no matter the church. The only requirement:

> *Slay the negative messaging that you were likely conditioned for and don't let that influence you. Pray where God would have you as a songwriter.*

Our God, Jesus Christ, from the Bible, is the center of all our decisions.

If you are a solo artist or are a member of a faith-based band, consider adding the skill set of congregational songwriting. This form of lyric crafting shows how to write songs for gatherings and to grab and hold the attention of, and involve, the listener. This way of writing may supplement your ministry.

If you are *any* type of songwriter called by God, consider learning the ways of congregational songwriting. See how to develop your call to serve the Lord and his people. Where does all this information lead? How can you discover the method in which you will live out your call? Get answers, starting with this book. I have written others on this path. The second in this series, and currently available: *The 5 Steps to Get Your Songs Heard.* The third and fourth in the series, which are in process: *The Proverbs 27.17 Song Critique Method* and *Fishing in Church,* along with the Songs4God. net Worship Songwriting Academy that will help guide the way.

> *How to be a worship songwriter? First, seek the face of Jesus and his unquestioned wisdom and undeniable life-giving counsel to understand.*

How to be a worship songwriter? First, seek the face of Jesus and his unquestioned wisdom and undeniable life-giving counsel to understand.

- Align your songwriting ministry with Jesus
  - Understand the concept of Fishing in Church
  - Say YES to God and decide to take measurable action to form your ministry

- Slay the negatives and learn who you are
- Take the songwriter personality test
  - To learn your strengths and weaknesses as a songwriter
  - So you can improve your skills
  - So you can be a valuable co-writer, contributing your best to the song
- Know your SHAPE
  - What are your spiritual gifts?
  - What are you passionate about?
  - Define your abilities and your skill set.
  - Seek to understand your personality.
  - List your experiences from work, volunteering, and life.
- Learn the Ways of the Holistic Songwriter
  - The 5 Disciplines of the Holistic Songwriter
- The Proverbs 27.17 Songwriting Tools
  - Know the heart of worship
  - The power of 1:1 songwriting time with God
  - See the connection between theology, worship and songwriting
  - Prosody begins with the lyric
  - *The Proverbs 27.17 Lyric Formula*
  - *The Proverbs 27.17 Melody Shape Tool*
  - The next-level Song Crafting Techniques
    - *The Proverbs 27.17 Song Critique Method* (and rewriting a lyric for the listener)
    - Re-writing
    - Co-writing
      - The 8 Ground Rules for Kingdom Co-writing
  - Share and build on public domain songs
- The Faith-based Songwriting Community

- The Faith-based Music Publishing Company

The primary goal is to make you a sought-after songwriter that can move confidently into the future knowing the ways of writing that connect with listeners, and how you can self-publish your songs to serve your church and community.

The second goal is to create an environment where multiple congregational songwriters can flourish. You can create a small or large songwriting community where like-minded writers will discover the power of the Proverbs 27:17 methodology. In this community you will learn that "as iron sharpens iron, so one person sharpens another." Together with other like-minded songwriters, you will magnify your songwriting results as a united body. You and your co-writers will write songs and deliver them to your local churches and to the wider world.

As a third goal, a faith-based music publishing company is born from the products of the songwriting community. This music publisher will exist solely to meet and expand upon the goals of the songwriting community. They will first market the songs to local churches and then to the wider world.

The faith-based songwriting community will become publisher members of CCLI and use their song database as the vehicle to market our work. Note: CCLI will not be promoting your songs, the organization will.

If you never get so far as to create a songwriting community or publishing company (small or large!), you will have at least received the most focused congregational songwriting education available and become a highly trained and sought-after songwriter.

9

The Songs4God.net Worship Songwriting Academy

Declare Your Purpose and Discover Your Manifesto

YOUR SONGWRITING FUTURE LOOKS BRIGHT. And I invite you to choose the Songs4God.net Worship Songwriting Academy, where I promise you will see the most comprehensive collection of worship songwriting instruction.

Songs4God.net Worship Songwriting Academy, the home for the education of the congregational songwriter and those who wish to support them, presents all the tools and topics needed for the advanced success of writing, publishing, and promoting congregational songs. You can watch the construction process of the academy, and you will eventually find a series of certified online courses at https://worshipsongwritingacademy.com.

ACCLAIMED CONGREGATIONAL SONGWRITER

The Songs4God.net Worship Songwriting Academy exists to create and nurture songwriters to write songs for the glory of God. The academy's primary goal is to help songwriters create congregational worship songs that propel others to worship at the foot of the cross of Jesus Christ.

You will learn what it means to align your ministry with Jesus, the philosophy of Fishing in Church, your strengths and weaknesses as a songwriter, the ways of the holistic songwriter, the heart of worship, 1:1 songwriting time with God, the unique connection between theology, worship, and songwriting; the custom lyric and melody and song critique methods, kingdom co-writing, and how to build upon public domain songs. This will prepare you to self-publish your songs so you can serve your church and community.

You will earn the title of Acclaimed Congregational Songwriter.

FAITH-BASED SONGWRITING COMMUNITY ADMINISTRATOR

The second goal is to create an environment where multiple congregational songwriters can flourish. You can create small or large songwriting communities to share what you have learned. The songwriting academy will show you how to administrate such an organization. This community will be a well-structured magnet for like-minded writers to join so they can discover the power of Proverbs 27:17:

As iron sharpens iron, so one person sharpens another.

We will see more victories as a team.

"For where two or three gather in my name, there I am with them." In Matthew 28:20, Jesus promises us his presence in the person and power of the Holy Spirit as together we align our lives with his will. We will write songs to be delivered to our local churches and learn the steps to share them with the wider world. This faith-based songwriting community has one goal: To nurture and be the champion for all Acclaimed Congregational Songwriters so they can achieve their goals.

You will learn how to reach out to songwriters to learn the ways of the small-church congregational songwriting revolution and how to build a songwriting organization sympathetic to their goals. You will understand how partnerships flourish between the songwriting organization and worship leaders and pastors. The design of the workshops and community meetings will allow continued education in each of the areas mentioned above for the Acclaimed Congregational Songwriter. There will also be songwriting community administration management sessions, song critique forums, open mic sessions, songwriter break-out sessions, and song promotion forums. You will invite guest speakers and manage songwriting community membership.

You will earn the title of Faith-based Songwriting Community Administrator.

FAITH-BASED MUSIC PUBLISHING COMPANY ADMINISTRATOR

A Faith-based music publishing company is born from the products of the songwriting community. This music publisher will exist exclusively to meet and expand upon the goals of the songwriting community by first marketing their songs to local churches and then to the wider world.

The songwriting academy will provide the fundamentals, the details, and the philosophy so you create a music publishing organization with one goal: To help fulfill the mission statement of the songwriting organization. You will learn about songwriting administration, artist relations, songwriter's publishing rights, songwriter royalties, and the legal responsibilities of everyone so you can continue the education for your songwriters.

You will earn the title of Faith-based Music Publishing Company Administrator.

The Goals

The overall goal for the academy isn't to promote the creation of one large songwriting community or music publishing company. It is to show you how to become a unique songwriter, ready to create your own songwriting community and build your own music publishing company so you can carry forth the *local song theology* philosophy. These can be small or large organizations that serve church communities with fresh worship songs and distribute your songs around the world.

Initial revenue and song distribution for your new songwriting company will come from publisher membership in CCLI. The individual songwriter could already have a membership with them, or your faith-based music organization can represent them with their membership, depending on how you build your company. It is worth noting again: CCLI will not be promoting your songs, you will.

THE SONGS4GOD.NET SONGWRITING ACADEMY CURRICULUM

- Align your songwriting ministry with Jesus
  - Understand the concept of Fishing in Church
  - Say YES to God and decide to take measurable action to form your ministry
- Slay the negatives and learn who you are
- Take the songwriter personality test
  - To learn your strengths and weaknesses as a songwriter
  - So you can improve your skills
  - So you can be a valuable co-writer, contributing your best to the song
- Know your SHAPE
  - What are your spiritual gifts?
  - What are you passionate about?
  - Define your abilities and your skill set.
  - Seek to understand your personality.
  - List your experiences from work, volunteering, and life.
- Learn the Ways of the Holistic Songwriter
  - The 5 Disciplines of the Holistic Songwriter
- The Proverbs 27.17 Songwriting Tools
  - Know the heart of worship

- o The power of 1:1 songwriting time with God
- o See connection between theology, worship and songwriting
- o Prosody begins with the lyric
- o *The Proverbs 27.17 Lyric Formula*
- o *The Proverbs 27.17 Melody Shape Tool*
- o The next-level Song Crafting Techniques
  - *The Proverbs 27.17 Song Critique Method* (and rewriting a lyric for the listener)
  - Re-writing
  - Co-writing
    - The 8 Ground Rules for Kingdom Co-writing
- o Share and build on public domain songs
- The Faith-based Songwriting Community
- The Faith-based Music Publishing Company

The Songs4God.net Worship Songwriting Academy exists to:

1. *Create dedicated congregational songwriters* using the concepts, tools, and formulas from the above list and to declare their readiness to the world
2. *Educate and prepare association administrators* so they can form songwriting communities to serve, nurture, and promote congregational songwriters
3. *Educate and prepare music publishing administrators* so they can serve, nurture, and promote faith-based songwriting communities

The academy will teach all three tracks—Acclaimed Congregational Songwriter, Faith-based Songwriting Community Administrator, Faith-based Music Publishing

Company Administrator—simultaneously. A person can sign up for any individual track or choose a package of tracks.

If you have interest in the curriculum, would like to follow the progress, or want more information visit https://worshipsongwritingacademy.com.

This is the vehicle for the Small-church Congregational Songwriting Revolution. Read more about the basic philosophy and tools in the second book in this series, *The Five Steps to Get Your Songs Heard,* available at https://getyoursongsheard.com.

Visit https://getyoursongsheard.com to see all my books and receive a deep discount just because you downloaded this one.

Thank you for supporting my efforts and for supporting quality congregational songwriting! Pray for churches and songwriters in your community and around the world. Help to promote local song theology.

> *Pray for churches and songwriters in your community and around the world. Help to promote local song theology.*

Courtesy of Shutterstock

Pray for churches and for local song theology around the world

About the Author

Stephen Robert Cass is a hack golfer who aims for high mediocrity. Because of his lofty goals on the course, he may one day enter charity tournaments so he can donate his time and talents. When not swinging for the fences, he's known for:

- 50+ years as a worship musician and team member,
- 14 years as a worship leader,
- 27 years as a published Christian songwriter,
- 15 album projects, whether solo, produced or musician credits,
- 70+ worship song titles found at CCLI under the Solid Walnut Music catalog and Stephen Robert Cass.

Solid Walnut Music has given away original music CDs to Christian radio stations all over the world: the US, Canada, Mexico, Australia, England, Ireland, Russia, Ethiopia, Bulgaria, Italy, South Africa, South Korea, and Israel.

Go to https://getyoursongsheard.com, so your friends can receive this book plus bonuses.

Visit https://books2read.com/stephenrobertcass to find where his books are available.

See https://stephenrobertcass.com for all other e-book releases, the press kit, and speaking engagements.

Swing by https://songs4god.net for songwriting blogs and other information about Steve.

Please leave a review of this book at your favorite bookstore. Contact steve@songs4god.net.

Get more information about congregational songwriting at https://worshipsongwritingacademy.com.